The critics report on *The State of the Union*:

"Wins by a landslide. A good play, perfectly cast, with wonderfully funny lines and situations."

—Nichols, *Times*

"The smash hit for which the theatrical season has been waiting. A very funny, very serious, very welcome play."

—Garland, *Journal-American*

"Witty, wise and bright, a satire of the most devastating kind."

—Rascoe, *World-Telegram*

"An adult, witty play."

—Chapman, *News*

"*State of the Union* speaks out loud about things that need stating. A shining show, eloquent and engaging. A happy combination of wit and sense."

—Barnes, *Herald Tribune*

"Gets something said that greatly needs to be said."

—Kronenberger, *PM*

STATE OF THE UNION

STATE OF THE UNION

---★---

A COMEDY BY

HOWARD LINDSAY AND
RUSSEL CROUSE

WITH A FOREWORD BY

THOMAS L. STOKES

RANDOM HOUSE · NEW YORK

Photographs by courtesy of Vandamm Studio

FOREWORD

We are in that post-war era about which so much was said
and written when we were besieged on every side by war.

It all happened sooner than we expected. The change of
scenery and atmosphere was quick, hardly longer than an in-
termission in the theatre. One day the Army and Navy and
Marines still were fighting across the vast map of the Pacific.
The next day we were at peace.

We did not find the dream world that some had pictured
to us or that we had nurtured in our imagination. It was the
same old world, only cluttered up with more problems, deso-
lated by ruins, saddened by wrecked and ruined lives. Now
that the tense excitement of sacrifice was over, like a high
fever that subsides and leaves the body weak and exhausted,
we discovered that getting well and getting readjusted loomed
before us drearily. The tendency is to turn over, pull up
the covers, and forget if possible in sleep, even if fitful and
disturbed by bad dreams. We don't want to face our problems, and any mention of them irritates us, so that we strike
out angrily at everything about us. We find ourselves in a
generally bad humor.

But the time comes when we must get up and be about
our business.

That's a good time to take a look at ourselves.

We've been through something rather horrible and we

don't want ever to go through with it again, we and millions of others in the world.

It's worth a few minutes of contemplation of ourselves in the mirror, after first making ourselves comfortable in our lounging robe and with a steaming cup of coffee and a cigarette so that we can do a little serious thinking in pleasant surroundings before we get up and get about the world's work. For the things we are going to think about are not altogether pleasant. But we must ponder them honestly, checking backward to see how we came to our sorry state, admitting all the mistakes, the little sins and the big sins, the prejudices, the hates and, above all, the selfishness.

It is good if we can see ourselves so plainly that we can smile understandingly, if somewhat wryly, at the man or woman there in the mirror.

That is the honesty that is the beginning of wisdom.

We need it very much, all of us, all over this country, all over the world.

For we are in a moment of history that may very well decide whether we are fit people to live in the world that we have created, or whether we are hell-bent upon destroying ourselves and all the beautiful things we have fashioned.

State of the Union gives us that look at ourselves, the understanding look, the look that makes us laugh at ourselves and at the same time fear for ourselves unless we change ourselves and our ways.

It's a healthy and enjoyable experience that is provided us by Howard Lindsay and Russel Crouse. They parade us across the stage, analyze us, dissect us, with penetrating humor and sympathy.

State of the Union is a play about politics, but we are all
in it, because we are all in politics, whether we know it or
not. Politics is the art of governing ourselves. This play makes
us realize that we are all a part of politics, that we are all
responsible for governing ourselves, that we ought to recog-
nize this responsibility and do something about it. That is
essential, not only for ourselves in this particular union which
we call the United States, but for the union of all nations,
for we have accepted our obligations in that bigger union,
too. It is the responsibility of each of us to play our parts in
both of these unions. We have become, whether we realize
it fully or not, responsible citizens of the world. The war did
that.

State of the Union is not an allegory, but a highly enter-
taining play, moving swiftly from beginning to end. Yet it
is an allegory in a way, without ever suggesting it, as we
know after we have sat through it.

Grant Matthews, who is induced into an ambition to be
President, is essentially every one of us who wants something
or other in this world. Like the rest of us, he is pulled this
way and that by those who would have him achieve his ambition for their own selfish or unselfish ends. He is our own
conscience, fighting with itself.

The political boss who sees in him a likely instrument to
work his own way back to power wants him to compromise,
to straddle the issues in a way not to offend anybody, to ex-
ploit the passions and prejudices once again inflamed with
the return of peace. So does his mistress, publisher of a chain
of newspapers. It won't hurt, they argue seductively, for him
to compromise his principles temporarily so that he can get

to the White House. Then, naturally, he can be his own man.

The problem of this business man who would be President is the problem faced by any candidate for the Presidency, as for other political office, high or low. It is the problem that will be faced by candidates for the nominations to the Presidency in 1948, which makes an appreciation of it so necessary for all of us, citizens and voters, in order that we may know what is involved in the choice and choose as wisely as we can. Thus we may help to raise the standard, and thus only can we hope to raise the standard. It is not a law of the land that we in this country shall forever accept imitations and substitutes in those who govern us.

The better instincts of most of us, the deep-down desire to follow the honest way, to resist compromise, are represented by Grant's wife who finally triumphs in the struggle for his soul with a stirring plea that we must think of the next generation rather than the next election. Thereby she concentrates the whole problem that confronts us in this, the atomic age. Her husband throws his ambition, now a tarnished bauble, back into the faces of those who would use him, and in that defiant challenge he leaves us with a hope that in this way he may win out eventually, for that is the way we all want.

The play reflects the disintegrations and confusions of the post-war period, the pulling at cross purposes by all sorts of economic and social groups completely absorbed in their own selfish aims. It is a powerful appeal for us to get together as a people and as a nation, so that we may meet our problems and those of the world in a spirit of team play, of co-operation, of unity and, above all, with tolerance of each other. It shows how the nation can be divided by scheming politicians and political and other groups who play on the selfish instincts. It deplores a common practice by both political parties in trying to capitalize politically upon those who have heritages and backgrounds in other countries by setting them apart and appealing to their original nationalism, as Irish-Americans or Italian-Americans or Polish-Americans, and so on, instead of thinking of them as Americans, and letting them think of themselves as Americans. It reveals the danger of creating suspicion of our war allies, big and little.

In all of these ways we can lose the peace here at home and in the rest of the world.

We get here full warning of the cleverness with which the politician can dupe us, and see how easy it is to fall into the habit of letting him handle our affairs for us without much questioning. We are shown how much we are to blame in all of this.

The political boss who moves through the play has the ingratiating charm of most political bosses, and is sweetly reasonable, completely disarming in his amiable compromises and his intellectual dishonesties. The secondary political personages, his lieutenants and handmaidens, are those familiar at every party caucus or national convention. It is just as if you had wandered in upon a conversation in the lobbies of Congress, or been admitted to a gathering of political leaders plotting, in their practical way, how to lull the people in the next election and accomplish their designs and the designs of their masters, for as we see in this play they are the instruments of others, themselves. It is disturbing to learn how little the average citizen and voter has so often to do with all of this. But that is the way it is, and it is about time to begin to do something about it.

THOMAS L. STOKES

State of the Union was produced by Leland Hayward at the Hudson Theatre, New York City, on the night of November 14, 1945, with the following cast:

[In the order in which they speak]

JAMES CONOVER	*Minor Watson*
SPIKE MACMANUS	*Myron McCormick*
KAY THORNDYKE	*Kay Johnson*
GRANT MATTHEWS	*Ralph Bellamy*
NORAH	*Helen Ray*
MARY MATTHEWS	*Ruth Hussey*
STEVENS	*John Rowe*
BELLBOY	*Howard Graham*
WAITER	*Robert Toms*
SAM PARRISH	*Herbert Heyes*
SWENSON	*Fred Ayres Cotton*
JUDGE JEFFERSON DAVIS ALEXANDER	*G. Albert Smith*
MRS. ALEXANDER	*Maidel Turner*
JENNY	*Madeline King*
MRS. DRAPER	*Aline McDermott*
WILLIAM HARDY	*Victor Sutherland*
SENATOR LAUTERBACK	*George Lessey*

Staged by Bretaigne Windust
Settings by Raymond Sovey
Gowns by Hattie Carnegie

xi

SCENES

ACT ONE

Scene I—The study in James Conover's home in Washington, D. C.

Scene II—A bedroom in the Conover home. The following evening.

ACT TWO

The living room of a suite in the Book-Cadillac Hotel, Detroit. Several weeks later.

ACT THREE

Scene I—The living room of the Matthews' apartment in New York. Two weeks later.

Scene II—The same—an hour later.

ACT ONE

ACT ONE

Scene I

The study in the home of JAMES CONOVER *in Washington, D. C. It is a wood-paneled library. There is a recessed window upstage, with the curtains drawn. The wall brackets and lamps are lighted. There is a large desk at the right of the room and several easy chairs. At the left of the room there is a table on which stands a tray containing bottles of liquor, soda, glasses and a container filled with ice cubes.*

Four persons are seated in the room: JAMES CONOVER, *a quiet-spoken man of about 60, not quite the type the audience would expect as a politician.* MRS. KATHERINE THORNDYKE, *known hereafter as* KAY, *a handsome woman in her late thirties, the kind you would find talking to men more often than women.* SPIKE MACMANUS, *who has been for years a Washington political reporter, pudgy and genial and with a rough charm.* GRANT MATTHEWS, *a distinguished-looking man in his middle forties, a successful business man, but also much more than that.*

JAMES CONOVER *is seated to the right of his desk engaged in a telephone conversation. His share of the conversation consists almost entirely of listening, with an occasional murmur of assent. The other three are obviously waiting for him to finish. Their attention wanders away from* CONOVER *to themselves.* KAY *consults her handbag mirror and passes her hand over her hair.* GRANT *takes a fresh cigarette and lights it from the one he is about to discard.* SPIKE *takes a paper out of his*

3

pocket, glances at some notes on it and puts it back. KAY *looks toward* GRANT *and, when their eyes meet, she smiles and nods an indication that everything is going all right.*

In reply GRANT *shrugs noncommittally. They both look at* SPIKE, *who makes a reassuring gesture with his hands, palms down.*

CONOVER *interrupts the flow of conversation coming from the other end of the telephone, speaking with quiet authority.*

CONOVER
(*Into telephone*)

Dave, I'm sorry, but I have to give the Senator a free hand in this. (*Pause*) Has this occurred to you? The reason you and the Senator are fighting over this one appointment is because we lost the last election and the one before that and the one before that! We have to win the next one! The Senator feels that appointment will strengthen the party in his district. So there's no argument. (*Short pause*) Certainly, any time. Good night, Dave. (*He hangs up and turns to the others.*)

SPIKE

You're being pretty tough on Tisdale, Jim. If he can't swing that appointment, how's he going to stay out of jail?

CONOVER

Spike, you know too much.

SPIKE
(*Grinning*)

I've been blackmailing Tisdale for years. He's one of my best sources.

CONOVER

Spike's just trying to show off in front of his boss, Mrs. Thorndyke.

KAY

He doesn't have to. I'm not the only publisher who thinks Spike's the best newspaper man in Washington.

CONOVER

Well, I think Walter Lippmann writes a little better.

KAY

Oh, we wouldn't let Spike write a paragraph. .

SPIKE

They even took away my typewriter—but they gave me six telephones.

KAY

Spike knows more about what's going on in Washington than you and Bob Hannegan put together. That's why I'm willing to lend him to you for the campaign—but I want him back!

CONOVER

(*Half kidding*)

Too bad you weren't running Dewey's campaign, Spike.

SPIKE

Well, if Dewey had listened to me when I saw him in Pawling he'd have had a much better chance. (*The others look at* SPIKE *with smiling disbelief*) I didn't say he'd have had a *chance*. I said he'd have had a much better chance.

5

KAY

(*To* CONOVER)

Jim, do you think you're going to have trouble stopping Dewey?

CONOVER

(*Quietly*)

He's built up a strong organization. But I think it can be done. That's why we have to start early.

SPIKE

The Republicans never have nominated a defeated candidate. That's on the record. The boys feel that way about Dewey, don't they, Jim?

CONOVER

I can't speak for the Republican Party . . .

SPIKE

Hell, who can these days? But, Jim, you're certainly strong enough to stop anyone on the horizon now. So why can't you name your own man?

KAY

If we get a strong candidate in '48 we've got better than a fighting chance. Jim, my newspapers are city papers, but small cities, with a rural circulation too. They make a pretty good sounding board. Here's what comes back to me. The party's best chance in '48 is to put up a candidate who's never been identified with politics.

SPIKE

Look what happened in '40. If the election had been held a month after Philadelphia, Willkie would have won.

KAY

Yes, and why? Because the people had the idea Willkie was someone you politicians didn't want.

SPIKE

(*To* CONOVER)

You wouldn't mind if that impression got around about the candidate in '48, would you?

CONOVER

Not if the candidate was someone I *did* want.

SPIKE

That's what I mean.

CONOVER

It seems to me at this point we ought to hear from Mr. Matthews.

(*They all look at* GRANT.)

GRANT

Let me make this clear—I don't want to be President of the United States.

(*They smile at his vehemence.*)

7

CONOVER

That decision may not be in your hands.

GRANT

Mr. Conover, I can understand Mrs. Thorndyke telling me I should be President. But you—you must be talking about somebody else.

CONOVER

You're a national figure—and you have been ever since the war started.

SPIKE

Is Henry Kaiser a national figure? For every ship he's built you've built a hundred planes.

KAY

Grant, everybody in the country knows you and everybody respects you.

GRANT

Oh, they know I make good airplanes and I've made a hell of a lot of them.

SPIKE

They know more than that. (*He rises and goes to* GRANT) When you fought the aluminum combine! When you slugged it out with the War Production Board until they broke those bottlenecks! The time you talked back to that Senate Investigating Committee! Three times you crowded the war off the front page!

CONOVER

Mrs. Thorndyke and I aren't the only Republicans who've been thinking about you. Those speeches you've been making —especially that last one in Cleveland.

GRANT

(Putting his glass down on the table)

When I made that speech in Cleveland I was trying to put both parties on the spot. I wasn't speaking as a Republican. I was speaking as a citizen. (*He rises and moves toward* CONOVER, *as he warms to his subject*) I'm worried about what's happening in this country. We're splitting apart. Business, labor, farmers, cattlemen, lumbermen—they're all trying to get the biggest bite of the apple. We talk about the war being over—well, we've got a war on here at home now—a civil war—an economic war. That's what I said in Cleveland. That's why I was surprised you asked me down here.

CONOVER

Why were you surprised?

GRANT

Because you politicians are trying to make capital out of this situation—you appeal to each one of these pressure groups just to get their votes. But let me tell you something. I don't think that's good politics. A lot of people wrote me after that speech in Cleveland. (*With a grin*) Of course I will admit that the business men liked best what I said about labor, and the unions said I was absolutely right about big business, and the farmers were pretty pleased with what I said about everybody but the farmers. (*He becomes serious again*) But they all knew what I was talking about. They know we've all got to work in harness, if we're going to take our place in this world. And if we don't there won't be any world. We may be kidding ourselves that our party is going to win in

9

'48—that the people here will want a change the way they did in England—but if our party does win, whoever is President has to have guts enough to pull us together and keep us together. I'm for that man, Mr. Conover—I don't care who he is.

KAY

That man is you, Grant.

GRANT

You're prejudiced, Kay. (*To* CONOVER) The boys who are back from fighting the war deserve something better . . .

(*There is a knock on the door.*)

CONOVER

Go ahead, finish.

GRANT

No, that may be important.

CONOVER

Come in.

(NORAH, *a middle-aged maid, wearing glasses, enters. She has a slip of paper in her hand.*)

NORAH

I'm sorry to interrupt you. It's a telephone call. (*She hands* CONOVER *the slip of paper. He looks at it.*)

CONOVER

Thank you. You go to bed, Norah. I'll take the rest of the calls myself.

NORAH

(*Starting out*)

Thank you, Mr. Conover. (*Turns back at the door*) It's turned cool. I've put an extra blanket in your room, Mrs. Thorndyke. Yours, too, Mr. Matthews.

GRANT

Thank you, Norah. Good night.

KAY

Good night, Norah.

(NORAH *exits*.)

CONOVER

Do you mind? I'll try to make this short. (*He picks up telephone and speaks into it*) Hello, there! How are you? (*Pause*) Oh—can you call me on that in the morning? (*Pause*) Well, hold on. I'll have to take this in another room. Spike MacManus is here.

(CONOVER *rises, holding the telephone.* SPIKE *crosses to the desk, reaching for the telephone.*)

SPIKE

I'll hang up as soon as you're on.

11

CONOVER

(*Giving him a look, then extending the telephone to* KAY)

Mrs. Thorndyke, do you mind? Spike has a little Drew Pearson blood. (CONOVER *exits.*)

SPIKE
(*To* KAY)

If he doesn't want me to hear that, it's something we ought to hear.

(*There is a long pause,* KAY *holding the receiver to her ear.*)

KAY
(*Watching* SPIKE, *but speaking into the telephone*)

Are you on? All right, I'll hang up. (*To amuse* SPIKE *she listens for a moment before putting the receiver down.* GRANT *has been pacing the room nervously.* SPIKE *sits in* CONOVER'S *chair and picks up a volume of* Who's Who *that is on* CONOVER'S *desk and opens it.*)

GRANT

I've never felt so uncomfortable in my life. When he comes back, I'm going to tell him to drop the whole subject.

KAY
(*Going to* GRANT)

I didn't come all the way to Washington to tell Jim Conover not to talk about something we came down here to talk about.

12

GRANT

(*Taking* KAY's *hands in his*)

Now, Kay, we had a lot of fun between ourselves dreaming about all this—but damn it, to ask a man like Conover to take it seriously . . .

KAY

(*Pushing* GRANT *into his chair*)

Now behave yourself. Mr. Conover and I are going to talk about you and you're going to sit right down and listen.

(GRANT *looks up and grins.*)

GRANT

All right, I'll listen. But if Conover is serious about considering me, the Republican Party must be pretty desperate.

SPIKE

(*Looking up from the book*)

You're damn right they're desperate!

GRANT

But Conover—he's always played along with the reactionaries. Why should he be interested in me?

SPIKE

If Conover isn't the guy who picks the Republican candidate for '48, he might as well turn Democrat.

KAY

You know, Grant, the last thing he has to boast about is Warren Harding.

(SPIKE *is studying the book in his lap.*)

13

SPIKE

And don't think he isn't serious about you! There was a bookmark in this *Who's Who* at your page. You know this even impresses me. (*He runs his finger down a page*) Twelve boards of directors! Say, there's a lot of swell angles about you! For instance, Honorary President of the Society for the Preservation of Wild Life. (*He puts the book back on the desk*) How can we use that in the campaign?

KAY

Spike, I don't think the wild-life vote is very important.

SPIKE

No, I mean from a publicity angle. Say, for instance, a picture in *Life*. (*He points to* GRANT) You and a grateful duck.

(CONOVER *enters.*)

CONOVER

After that call I need a drink.

SPIKE

(*Pointing to the telephone*)

Oh, Senator Taft!

CONOVER

(*Laughs, then turns to mix a drink*)

Anyone else?

14

SPIKE

I'll tend bar. (SPIKE *mixes drinks and serves them during the following.*)

CONOVER

Oh, thank you.

KAY

(*To* CONOVER)

Jim, do you think Taft's serious about being a candidate himself?

CONOVER

You can always figure that Senator Taft is serious. (*He returns to his chair and sits*) He'll go into the convention with Ohio and some Southern delegations.

GRANT

Don't kid yourselves. Truman isn't going to be easy to beat. He's made some strong appointments.

KAY

He's also made some weak ones.

CONOVER

Those are the ones that interest me—the weak ones. Between now and the campaign the Administration can run into some ugly trouble.

SPIKE

Well, all we can do is hope. (*He places drinks in front of* KAY *and* CONOVER.)

KAY

Jim, Labor's already asking Truman for more than he can give them. I think we've got a chance for the labor vote if we have the right candidate.

SPIKE

That rules out Sewell Avery!

KAY

But it doesn't rule out Grant. (*She rises*) No employer in the country's got a better labor record. And business is bound to go along with him. Jim, don't you see the strength we have in Mr. Matthews? Phil Murray and Sewell Avery would both vote for him.

GRANT

I'm not so sure—because I wouldn't promise either one of them anything.

SPIKE

You'd have to promise them something. (*He hands* GRANT *a drink and pauses for thought*) Still, Dewey outpromised Roosevelt and it didn't get him anywhere.

GRANT

That's one of our most serious problems. There's not enough difference between the two parties.

SPIKE

Well, not to change the subject, I would like to pause at this moment and take a one-man Gallup poll. What do you think of Mr. Matthews' chances, Jim?

CONOVER

That's not an easy question to answer. I haven't got much to go on. After Mr. Matthews makes his speech here Monday night I'd know a little more about what the feeling is here in Washington. Is Mrs. Matthews coming down to hear you speak?

GRANT

(*Amiably*)

No, she takes bringing up the children more seriously than she does my speeches. And I think she's right. This has all been very flattering—but as I said to Mrs. Thorndyke while you were out of the room—let's drop the whole idea.

KAY

(*Quickly. To* CONOVER)

Jim, Tuesday Grant's starting a tour of his plants. Everywhere he's going he's been invited to speak.

SPIKE

Minneapolis, Seattle, San Francisco, Los Angeles, Denver, Wichita, Detroit—

KAY

If Grant made those speeches, at the end of the tour could you tell him whether he had a chance, or whether we should give up the whole idea?

CONOVER

(*With a little thought*)

That covers a lot of territory. Yes, I think if Mr. Matthews made those speeches I could be pretty definite.

17

KAY

(*Going to* GRANT)

Grant, you've got to go along with us that far! You've got to make those speeches!

GRANT

(*Looking up at* KAY)

Kay, I'm going to be pretty busy on this trip. I've got problems in every one of those plants. I've got to do my damnedest to keep those men working. Besides, I wish I knew how much you had to do with those invitations for me to speak.

KAY

(*Decisively*)

Spike, you're going to make the trip with him. You've been telling everyone for years how to run a political campaign. Now we'll find out whether you can run one. The bureau can get along without you for a couple of weeks. It will be a vacation for you.

CONOVER

It will be a vacation for everyone in Washington. (*Briskly*) Now that we've reached that decision, there's a lot for all of us to talk about. On this tour, Mr. Matthews . . . (*Telephone rings*) Damn! Pardon me! (CONOVER *answers the telephone*) Hello. (*With some interest*) Oh, yes, I've been waiting to hear from you. (*Looks around room unhappily*) Hold on. Wait a minute. (*He rises*) Spike, why don't you go home? (*He hands the telephone to* KAY) Do you mind, Mrs. Thorndyke?

KAY

(*Rises and takes the telephone*)

I'm glad you trust publishers.

CONOVER

(*Going to the door*)

Just Republican publishers.

SPIKE

I thought it was agreed we were all to trust each other.

CONOVER

Only when we're in the same room. (*He exits.*)

SPIKE

(*Gleefully rubbing his hands*)

Mr. Conover has just leaped gracefully onto the front seat of the bandwagon.

GRANT

Take it easy, Spike. Conover hasn't brought up the payoff yet.

SPIKE

Well, there's one promise I want.

GRANT

What?

SPIKE

That I'm not to be the next Postmaster General.

GRANT

I'll settle for that, Spike—you're not the next Postmaster
General. And that's the only commitment I'm going to make.

SPIKE

You settled awfully quick. I just threw that in for a laugh.
(*He turns to* KAY) Mrs. Thorndyke—tell Sir Galahad
here . . .

KAY

(*Into the telephone*)
Are you on? All right, I'll hang up. (*Again to amuse* SPIKE,
*she keeps her ear to the receiver. Suddenly her expression
changes sharply. She presses down the disconnector with her
free hand, then releases it immediately and continues to listen
in, giving the men a warning gesture.* GRANT *rises indignantly
and starts toward her.*)

GRANT

Kay!

(SPIKE *stops him with a gesture.* GRANT *obviously dis-
approves and walks unhappily away, as if he will have
none of it.* SPIKE *beams in admiration of* KAY *at first,
but as she listens in and flashes a look toward* GRANT,
SPIKE *realizes it is a serious matter and his smile van-
ishes. Even* GRANT'S *attention is arrested. The two men
stand watching* KAY. *She hangs up and goes immediately to* GRANT, *speaking quickly and with deep con-
cern.*)

KAY

It's a report from New York. He's had someone looking you up. They've picked up some gossip about you and me.

SPIKE

Oh—oh!

KAY

And there's been talk about Mary, too—Mary and some Major.

SPIKE

Who's Mary?

KAY

Mrs. Matthews.

SPIKE

Oh—ho!

GRANT

What Major? What's his name?

KAY

I couldn't get his name.

GRANT

What'd the name sound like?

(KAY *gestures to him to be quiet*.)

KAY

Sh-h. He'll be back in a minute. (*She raises her voice, making a pretense of normal conversation*) Of course, Spike, that's one way of looking at it, but you never can be sure.

GRANT
(*Sitting down*)

A Major!

SPIKE
(*To* GRANT *as* CONOVER *enters*)
On the other hand, if what you say is true, Mr. Matthews,
that makes the migratory flamingo a very interesting bird.

CONOVER
What makes the flamingo an interesting bird, Spike?

SPIKE
(*Caught short, but not very*)
Tell him what you just told us, Mr. Matthews.

GRANT
(*At no loss whatever*)
I don't think Mr. Conover's interested in the wild life
of America.

CONOVER
Staying up this late is a little more wild life than I'm used
to. I think we'd better call it a night.

(*They are caught flatfooted by his tone of dismissal.*)

SPIKE
(*Tentatively*)
Nothing else you want to bring up, Jim?

CONOVER

Not now. (GRANT *rises*) Spike, you may have a little trouble getting a taxi. Good night. (CONOVER *shakes hands with* SPIKE.)

SPIKE

Good night, Jim. Good night, Boss. (*He turns to* GRANT) Grant, if the lights are still on in the White House, I'll drop in and tell the Trumans to start packing.

KAY

Spike, you'd better get off some wires accepting those speaking dates for Grant.

CONOVER

I'd like to give some of those cities a little more thought. (SPIKE *gets his hat and crosses to the door*) Tomorrow's time enough for that, isn't it?

GRANT

Yes—I guess so. (*He goes to* CONOVER) Well, Mr. Conover, if I never get any closer to the White House than this, it's been a very pleasant evening. I'll say good night, too.

CONOVER

You and I might take time to finish our drinks.

KAY

I haven't finished mine— (*No one asks her to stay*) I'll finish it in my room. (*She starts to rise, picking up her bag and drink.*)

CONOVER

I thought Mr. Matthews and I might chat for a few minutes longer.

KAY

I'll run along then. I can't tell you how grateful we are for your having us here. Good night. Good night, Grant.

GRANT

Good night, Kay.

KAY

(*She starts to door, stops and turns back to* CONOVER; SPIKE *is holding door open for her*)
Jim, I want you to know how completely we trust you. (*She goes directly to* GRANT) Good night, darling. (*She puts her arms around him and they kiss. She starts out again.*)

CONOVER

Mrs. Thorndyke! (KAY *stops and turns*) You might as well finish your drink here. That's what I was going to talk about. (KAY *raises her eyebrows, comes back and sits down.* SPIKE *closes the door, and drops his hat on a chair*) Naturally, Mr. Matthews, when your name first came up as a possible candidate, I made some inquiries. It seems there's been some talk about you and Mrs. Thorndyke.

GRANT

What kind of talk?

CONOVER

(*Easily*)
I think you know what I mean when I say talk.

24

KAY

We wouldn't pretend to deny there's basis for it, but it can't be very widespread.

GRANT

Kay, let Mr. Conover tell us what he's heard.

CONOVER

That's about all. There's been some gossip. That's nothing unusual, and as long as it's about a man who makes airplanes, even though you're very well known, I don't think it would spread a great deal, but the minute you become a public figure . . .

KAY

You think it might be used against Mr. Matthews?

CONOVER

Not openly. What it would come down to would be a whispering campaign.

GRANT

(*Firmly*)

Frankly, Mr. Conover, I don't give a damn for the kind of opinion that sort of thing would influence.

CONOVER

I haven't any respect for it, either; but I have to reckon with it. You see, Mr. Matthews, while Mrs. Thorndyke happens to be divorced, you're a married man.

GRANT

Well, if you think that's a major—(*His mind sticks mo-*

mentarily on the word)—a vital factor . . . Kay, that seems to settle it.

KAY

Wait a minute, Grant! Jim, there must be some way around this.

CONOVER

Yes, there's a very obvious one.

GRANT

So? What is it?

CONOVER

I'd like to see your wife with you when you speak here Monday night, and I'd like to see her make this trip with you.

GRANT

(*Laughing*)

That's not the solution. If Mary knew that I even thought of myself as President of the United States . . .

KAY

Jim, we've got to think of something else. It's a little difficult for me to talk about Mrs. Matthews in this situation but—you've seen the kind of wife—the more important her husband becomes the more determined she is to make him feel unimportant.

GRANT

Now, wait a minute, Kay! Be fair to Mary. (*To* CONOVER) I don't want you to get the wrong impression of my wife, Mr. Conover. She's no shrew. She's a damn bright woman.

KAY

Grant, you know Mary's always cutting you down.

GRANT

I can't deny that. Still, I suppose her criticism of me has been valuable sometimes. (*To* CONOVER) But a man does reach a saturation point.

CONOVER

If you become a candidate you'll have to take a lot of criticism.

SPIKE

Yes, your wife might be good training for you. Toughen you up.

KAY

I think it's more important that Grant should have his self-confidence.

CONOVER

(*Sitting on the edge of his desk*)

The most important thing of all is to kill this gossip. We haven't got a chance unless we do. The American people like to think of a married candidate as happily married. They want to see him and his wife together. They like to see them make the campaign together. It's an American tradition. You'd have to face that sooner or later. I think the sooner you face it the better.

GRANT

Yes, Mary may solve the whole situation for us. I'm not so sure she would campaign with me even if I asked her to.

CONOVER

Why don't you call her and find out?

(KAY *and* GRANT *exchange a look of mutual inquiry.*)

GRANT

(*To* CONOVER)

Why not? (CONOVER *picks up the telephone and dials.*)

SPIKE

There's been that gossip about every candidate except Herbert Hoover. They didn't pull it on Hoover because nobody would have believed it.

CONOVER

(*Into telephone*)

This is Dupont 4108. I want a New York call. I want to speak to Mrs. Grant Matthews at . . . (*He looks inquiringly at* GRANT.)

GRANT

Plaza 5-8249.

CONOVER

(*Into phone*)

Plaza 5-8249. (*He rises and hands the telephone to* GRANT) Invite her to stay here, of course.

GRANT

(*Taking the telephone*)

There's no way of a man being elected President before his wife hears about it, is there? (*He sits beside the desk*) Hello.

Well, put it through as soon as you can and call me. (*He hangs up and there is an uneasy pause. They are not looking at each other. Finally* SPIKE *speaks up brightly.*)

SPIKE

Shall we dance?

(JIM CONOVER *gives him a look that's an answer, but not to his question.*)

GRANT

Mr. Conover, I'm glad there's a delay in that call because before it comes through there's something I'd like to ask you.

CONOVER

Yes?

GRANT

If it works out that we can go ahead, you and I, what are you going to expect of me?

CONOVER

I'd expect you to be elected.

GRANT

Mr. Conover, I'm inexperienced in politics, but I am not—shall I say—completely naive. Let's put it this way—if I were elected, naturally I'd be very grateful to you. Is there any particular way in which you'd expect me to show my gratitude?

29

KAY

Grant, aren't you being a little premature? (*To* CONOVER) It's probably pre-natal influence. Grant was a premature baby.

SPIKE

You were? Say, drop that into an interview some time. There may be some votes in that. There are a lot of bastards who think they were seven-month babies.

CONOVER

In answer to your question, Mr. Matthews, if you mean have I a list of Federal appointments in my pocket?—No.

GRANT

I'd be very glad to see any list of names you wanted to show me. I just want it to be clear I'm not making any commitments.

CONOVER

I can't ask for more than an open mind. Mrs. Thorndyke said you two came down here for my advice. Well, politics is my business. If we do get into a campaign together I hope you'll be open-minded about any advice I might give you then.

GRANT

I'd welcome it—only I can't promise I'd always follow it.

KAY

Now, Grant, don't turn down advice before you get it.

GRANT

(*To* CONOVER, *with a disarming laugh*)
All right. Give me some!

CONOVER

(*Amused, but still serious*)
Well, in that list of speaking dates, you mentioned Minneapolis. I wouldn't speak there. You might just stir up trouble. That's Stassen territory. The local boys would resent it and you might start a backfire.

GRANT

That's damn good advice. I'll take it. How do you feel about Stassen?

CONOVER

There's a good deal of opposition to him in the party. Oh, that prompts me to venture some more advice, if you don't mind?

GRANT

No—shoot!

CONOVER

If you make this preliminary tour, keep whatever you have to say pretty general. Don't be too specific.

GRANT

There I'm afraid I can't go all the way with you. The only reason I have for speaking at all is because there are some things I feel deeply about.

KAY

Grant, it's only that at this early stage . . .

GRANT

No, Kay! I'm not going to pull any punches! I want that understood!

KAY

Grant, if you keep on being belligerent about your honesty, we'll begin to suspect you.

CONOVER

(*Serenely*)

Mr. Matthews, most candidates have to spend a lot of time explaining things they wish they hadn't said. You're not carrying that weight because you haven't said very much yet. Your danger at this point might be in raising minor issues that would come back to plague you later.

KAY

Grant, this isn't the airplane business. You're used to dealing with tangible things. I know what Jim's talking about because I have to go out after circulation. You'll have to go out after votes.

GRANT

Oh, I know you have to appeal for votes. But I think what I believe in . . .

(*The telephone rings.* SPIKE *picks it up.*)

32

SPIKE

(*Into telephone*)

Hello. New York? Just a minute. (*He hands the telephone to* GRANT. KAY *goes to a chair on the farther side of the room and sits.*)

GRANT

(*Into telephone*)

Hello. Hello. What's that? (*With a little impatience*) Well, get them back. No, I'll hang on.

CONOVER

Have you your speech for Monday night prepared?

GRANT

Yes. Want to look at it tomorrow? I'll listen to anything you have to say.

KAY

And on the tour you listen to Spike. He can be very valuable.

GRANT

(*Grinning*)

If I know Spike, he's going to give me plenty of advice.

SPIKE

No, Mr. Matthews, my big job is to humanize you.

GRANT

(*In amused surprise*)

Oh, is it?

SPIKE

I've got a lot of things dreamed up. Do you know what first sold Willkie to the country as a human being? His going on Information Please. He came over as a regular guy and he held his own, too.

GRANT

Just a minute! I'm no Wendell Willkie—I'm willing to take on Harry Truman, but not John Kieran.

SPIKE

We've got to do something to counteract those speeches.

GRANT

Counteract them! Well then, why am I making them?

SPIKE

Oh, no, you've got to make them. But sometimes your speeches get a little fancy. We don't want people to think you're stuffy.

GRANT

Do you know, Spike, you sound just like my wife. (*At this moment he hears his wife's voice on the telephone and speaks to her with some surprise*) Hello, Mary. (*Pause*) I'm in Washington. How's Joyce? (*Pause*) Doctor been there to-day? (*Pause*) That's fine . . . If she's that well, Sonny won't catch it now. (*Pause*) Mary, I'm making another speech down here Monday night. (*Pause—then somewhat indignantly*) No, they *asked* me to! I'd like to have you come down and listen to it, if it wouldn't bore you too much. (*Pause*) As a matter of fact, I won't *be* home for a few weeks. I'm making

a tour of the plants. How'd you like to make the trip with me?—I wish you would. We haven't made the circuit together in a long time. (*Pause*) But how about coming down here, anyway? We'll be house guests at Jim Conover's. (*Pause*) Conover—a friend of mine, but in spite of that you'll like him. (*Pause*) Get here tomorrow night— It doesn't matter how late. I'll send the plane back for you— Swell! (*Pause*) Bring enough clothes for the trip, anyway. We can talk it over when you get here. Mary, you'll need a dinner dress here Monday night. It's a banquet. (*Gaily*) You'll get my speech for dessert. (*Pause*) What? (*Not so gaily*) All right— Of course you'll look a little funny sitting there with earmuffs on. Good night. (*He hangs up*) I'm not sure the Presidency's worth it.

CONOVER

She's coming?

GRANT

Yes, Heaven help me.

KAY

Grant, you know what that means. If Mary's coming here I've got to go home tomorrow.

CONOVER

I confess that would ease the housing situation. The National Committee seems to think I run a hotel.

KAY

(*Starting for the door*)

Well, for the next few weeks I'll be sitting alone in New York, while you tour the country with your wife.

SPIKE

(*Thoughtfully*)

Politics makes strange bedfellows.

(KAY *looks at him sharply.* SPIKE *catches the look, picks up his hat and starts out of the room.*)

Curtain

ACT ONE

Scene II

The next night.

A bedroom in JIM CONOVER's *house. There is a double bed with bed tables on each side of bed. There are two over-stuffed chairs with a small table between them. The entrance to the bedroom is upstage to the left. There is a window downstage left. On the right there is a door leading to a dressing room and bathroom offstage. Below the door is a desk with a chair.*

GRANT, *wearing horn-rimmed glasses, is discovered alone, seated at the desk, editing the loose pages of his typewritten speech. There is a knock at the door.*

GRANT

(*Taking off his glasses*)

Come in!

(CONOVER *enters.*)

CONOVER

How's the speech coming along?

GRANT

All right, I guess. What Spike said last night had me worried. I'm trying to unfancy it a little bit.

37

CONOVER

Don't let Spike worry you. I think it's very good. When you finish, drop back downstairs. I think it would be a good idea to have the boys see as much of you as possible. You made a very good impression at dinner.

GRANT

I was thrown a little by the way Senator Fosdick kept yessing me. He's an America Firster, isn't he?

CONOVER

He was—until he was defeated. (*He starts to leave*) I'll see you later then. (*Turns back*) Oh! I came up to tell you I've sent the car down to the airport.

GRANT

(*Looking at his watch*)

He might have quite a wait. I don't think Mary will be in much before midnight. (*A little disturbed*) If she could have told me when she was getting in I could have met her myself.

(SPIKE *enters.*)

SPIKE

Jim, Governor Dunn just arrived.

CONOVER

(*To* GRANT)

Oh, that's fine! I want you to meet him. He can be very valuable to you in the Northwest. I'm glad he dropped in.

SPIKE

Like hell you are! He brought his bags with him.

CONOVER

Oh, damn! Where am I going to put him? Well, I guess I'll have to take him into my room, and I was hoping for a good night's sleep. Spike, you're an expert in these matters. Why do all Governors snore?

SPIKE

It's an occupational disease.

GRANT

Where are you putting Mary?

(CONOVER *is taken a little by surprise.*)

CONOVER

In here with you. If we're going to create the impression about you two that we want to, this would be a good start.

GRANT

(*Troubled*)

I don't think she'd welcome the idea. We rushed into this decision and it's been on my conscience ever since. Look, Jim, when Mary finds out what's up, she can still say no. But moving her in here with me tonight . . .

39

CONOVER

(*Thinking*)

Well, Senator Fosdick's room is about the only one. He's in there alone. But where can I put the Senator? There's nothing left but the billiard table.

SPIKE

Why not? The son-of-a-bitch didn't even carry his own state.

CONOVER

I'll put him on a cot somewhere. Come on down with me. I want you to meet the Governor.

SPIKE

He's got to finish that speech. I want to take it with me tonight.

GRANT

I'm almost through.

CONOVER

(*Turning at the door*)

Shall I send up a drink?

SPIKE

Send up a couple.

(CONOVER *exits*.)

GRANT

Why are you in such a hurry? There's plenty of time to get this copied before tomorrow night.

SPIKE

All the wire services will want it by noon, and even if they don't want it they're going to get it. If they don't have it in advance you may only get a couple of paragraphs. Are you out on a limb anywhere in here? (*He picks up first few pages of the manuscript and starts glancing through it*) Because we could play it the other way. Not give out any copies —then you could always claim you've been misquoted.

GRANT

I wish I was as sure as you seem to be that I'll be quoted at all.

SPIKE

This isn't as bad as I thought it was going to be.

GRANT

Those changes were all made for your benefit.

SPIKE

(*Placing one sheet in front of* GRANT)
This spot in here sounds a little like a speech. (*He points.*)

GRANT

Damn it!—It *is* a speech!

SPIKE

That's what I meant.

(*There is a knock on the door.*)

41

GRANT

Come in!

(NORAH *enters, loaded down with two bags and a hat-box.*)

NORAH

(*From doorway*)

These are Mrs. Matthews' bags.

GRANT

(*Rising*)

Oh, is my wife here?

NORAH

She just came. I'll put these in the dressing room.

(GRANT *stops her.*)

GRANT

No, they don't go there. Mrs. Matthews is in another room.

NORAH

(*Bewildered*)

What other room?

(CONOVER *enters.*)

CONOVER

Grant, Mrs. Matthews is here!

(MARY *follows* CONOVER *in.* MARY *is an attractive woman in her thirties, brisk and self-assured. She is dressed in a smart traveling suit and hat.*)

GRANT

Hello, dear.

MARY

Hello, Grant. (*She goes to* GRANT *and they kiss.*)

GRANT

I didn't expect you to get here this early.

MARY

I think we broke the record—and both my ear drums.

GRANT

Spike, I want you to meet Mrs. Matthews. (*To* MARY) This is Mr. MacManus.

MARY

How do you do, Mr. MacManus?

SPIKE

(*Standing near window*)

Hello, Mrs. Matthews.

GRANT

You seem to have met Mr. Conover.

MARY

Oh, yes, downstairs. (*She smiles at* CONOVER) It's so nice of you to have us here. I'm really quite excited. I hope you'll notice, Grant, I've packed for the whole trip. (*She points to the bags, which* NORAH *is still holding, then speaks to* NORAH) Just put those down anywhere.

43

NORAH

I was told you were going to be in another room. (NORAH *looks toward* CONOVER.)

CONOVER

Leave the bags here for a minute, Norah. You're moving Senator Fosdick.

NORAH

Again?

CONOVER

Put him in the south bedroom with Mr. Godfrey.

NORAH

The Commissioner's in there with Mr. Godfrey.

CONOVER

We have another cot, haven't we?

NORAH

That army cot.

MARY

That's nonsense. Don't move Senator Fosdick. Grant and I can stay here. (*She looks around at the group*) We're really married. (CONOVER *hesitates*) Unless the rest of the Senate is in here with Grant.

GRANT

Mr. Conover just thought you'd be more comfortable with a room to yourself.

MARY

(*To* NORAH)

I'll stay here. (NORAH *crosses to the dressing room with the bags.* GRANT *holds the door open for her.* MARY *goes to the bed and throws hat and bag on it. She starts removing her gloves*) After all, Senator Fosdick's an isolationist. I think he ought to be isolated.

SPIKE

(*Grinning*)

I'm going to like you.

(MARY *answers him with a smile.*)

NORAH

(*At dressing-room door*)

Shall I unpack for you, Ma'am?

MARY

Just the small bag. And you can take the shoes out of my hat box. (NORAH *starts out*) Oh, there's a print dress in the suitcase I'd like to wear tomorrow. Could it be pressed for me?

NORAH

Surely. (*She exits into the dressing room with the bags.*)

MARY

(*Pressing her ears*)

Those plane trips always leave me deaf.

45

GRANT

If that lasts through tomorrow you'll be spared hearing my speech.

MARY

(*Smiling at him*)
That's a little more than I could hope for.

(*The others are politely amused. There is a knock on the door.* STEVENS, *the butler, enters with two drinks on a tray. He's a little bewildered to find four people.*)

STEVENS

Scotch and soda?

MARY

I'm not as deaf as I thought I was. What a perfect host! (*She takes one of the highballs.*)

CONOVER

I'll take the other one, Stevens. (*To* GRANT) You and Spike get your drinks downstairs. I want you to meet the Governor.

(STEVENS *exits.*)

GRANT

Want to meet a Governor, Mary?

MARY

I'd like to get a little better acquainted with this highball.

46

CONOVER

That was my idea. You and I, let's finish our drinks quietly up here. (*To* GRANT) We'll join you later.

SPIKE

How about the rest of this Gettysburg Address? Finished with it?

GRANT

Yes, I think the end's all right. Take it along. (*He hands* SPIKE *his speech.*)

CONOVER

Spike, see that Grant and Governor Dunn get together.

SPIKE
(*Exiting*)

All right.

CONOVER

Grant, I'm sure the Governor will be very interested in meeting you.

GRANT
(*With a touch of self-importance*)

I'll be glad to talk to him. (GRANT *exits.* MARY *smiles at* CONOVER *and goes to one of the easy chairs and sits down.*)

MARY

This is very pleasant.

CONOVER

It is for me.

MARY

Now I can boast that I've really been behind the scenes in Washington.

CONOVER

You certainly can! The Republican Party's been behind the scenes for fourteen years. However, that's about over. I think we're going to win next time.

MARY

If I needed an excuse to drink, that would be it. (*She lifts her glass to* CONOVER. *They drink*) But you'll have to offer the Democrats a good reason for voting Republican.

CONOVER

Your husband's been lecturing me along those lines.

MARY

Then I'd better change the subject. Grant can be very outspoken—but not by anybody I know.

CONOVER

Everything he said about politicians we had coming to us. I have a great admiration for your husband.

MARY

I'm many years ahead of you on that.

CONOVER

Of course, everyone admires him as a business man. What impresses me is that he doesn't limit his thinking to his own field. (CONOVER *sits in the other easy chair*) He has a very clear vision about the whole country—what it needs—what the world needs. Any man who sees our problems as clearly as he does—it imposes on him a certain responsibility.

MARY

Oh, I think you're sure of a big check from him.

(CONOVER *smiles, then becomes serious.*)

CONOVER

No, I mean a responsibility to the country. I've been trying to persuade your husband to take an active part in the Government.

MARY

Mr. Conover, Grant's talking politics is one thing—but he has a big enough job ahead of him—that is, if you know anything about his plans for post-war aviation.

CONOVER

I don't think his usefulness should be limited to that. I think the country will feel that way, too, after hearing what he says here tomorrow night, and the speeches he's going to make on this trip.

MARY

Is he going to make speeches on the trip?

CONOVER

Yes, in several places.

MARY

(*Dismayed*)

Oh, dear. (*Catching herself*) Oh, I didn't mean that the way it sounded. Grant really can make a very good speech. But public appearances for me—I'm not good at that—I'm so uncomfortable. Would it be bad form if I just stayed quietly at the hotel and listened to him over the radio?

CONOVER

Yes, I'm afraid it would. It would defeat the whole purpose.

MARY

Purpose? What purpose?

CONOVER

(*Avoiding a direct answer*)

Mrs. Matthews, you must know how concerned your husband is about this country's splitting apart—how deeply he feels that it must be held together.

MARY

Oh, yes. We've been talking about it for months. Grant's been trying to figure out what could be done.

CONOVER

I think you can help him do something about it.

MARY

Oh, not me. I just get angry! I can't read the newspapers any more! While the war was on we were a united country—

50

we were fighting Germany and Japan. Now we're just fighting each other. No, I just get angry.

CONOVER

I'm glad you feel that strongly about it because it's important that wherever Grant goes now—wherever he makes these speeches—you're right there alongside of him.

(MARY *senses for the first time that there is more than meets the ear in* CONOVER'S *conversation.*)

MARY

Why should that be important?

CONOVER

(*Smoothly*)

Well, for a man who's going to be in the public eye—people like to know his wife—like to see what she looks like—like to see the two of them together.

MARY

(*Thoughtfully, putting her drink on the table*)

I was a little puzzled by Grant's invitation to make this trip with him.

CONOVER

Oh, Grant wants you to go along. These public appearances —they're my idea. It's just an old politician's habit of cashing in on an opportunity.

MARY

(*Rising and walking away*)

It all fits in a little too neatly, Mr. Conover. I don't know whether you know—(*She stops and looks at him sharply*) —or perhaps you do—that Grant and I haven't been very close for the last year or so.

CONOVER

Wouldn't you prefer to create a contrary impression?

MARY

Oh, then you do know! Let's be open about this. These public appearances that Grant and I are to make together— are they designed to kill off any talk about my husband and Mrs. Thorndyke?

CONOVER

There's that kind of talk about every important man. But if there are any rumors about your husband, this would be a good chance to kill them. (CONOVER *is watching* MARY *carefully*) You see, Mrs. Matthews . . .

(NORAH *enters from the dressing room, carrying a print dress.*)

NORAH

Is this the dress, Ma'am?

(MARY *stares at the dress and then comes to the surface.*)

MARY

Oh, yes. But don't bother to press it.

NORAH

It's no trouble at all, Ma'am. It won't take me long. I'll have it back tonight.

MARY

No! Please! (*But* NORAH *has gone.* MARY *to* CONOVER) May I use your telephone?

CONOVER

Certainly.

MARY

I want to get back to New York tonight if I can. (*She goes to the telephone, picks up the receiver and starts to dial.*)

CONOVER

(*Rising*)

Mrs. Matthews, I think any man who has a chance to become President of the United States deserves that chance.

(MARY *slowly puts down the telephone, turns and stares at* CONOVER *in astonishment.*)

MARY

President of the United States?

CONOVER

Yes. (*There is a short pause*) Don't you think he'd make a good President?

MARY

(*After consideration*)

Yes, I do.

CONOVER

Then you understand this goes beyond personal considerations. Let's not think of this in terms of you—and Grant—

MARY

—and Mrs. Thorndyke.

CONOVER

And Mrs. Thorndyke. I'm sure you will go along with us. You're a good citizen.

MARY

Right now, Mr. Conover, I'm not feeling like a good citizen! I'm feeling like a woman!

CONOVER

All right, as a woman!

MARY

As a woman, no, I won't go along with you. I resent being used!

CONOVER

Mrs. Matthews, let's think of it in terms of the country. That's what I've had to do. I am prepared to make some sacrifices.

MARY

(*Turning to him*)

What sacrifices?

CONOVER

Frankly, your husband isn't the kind of man a politician would prefer to deal with.

MARY

I've been wondering why any political party should choose Grant, knowing the things he stands for.

CONOVER

I want the people to make the choice.

MARY

That's damn white of you!

CONOVER

That's the purpose of this trip. I want the American people to get better acquainted with your husband. We don't know yet what's coming out of it, but I've told him that when this trip is over I can let him know whether to go ahead with the idea or forget the whole thing.

MARY

Oh, I don't think Grant could ever forget it. I'll bet he's running a pretty high fever right now. When he left the room I thought he walked as though he was trying to be two inches taller.

CONOVER

Mrs. Matthews, you see your husband at pretty close range. Take my word for it, he's a big man.

55

MARY

There's no argument about that, Mr. Conover. I know he's a big man and you know he's a big man. My bad days are when *he* knows he's a big man! (*She thinks for a moment*) You don't suppose there's any way of Grant being elected President and keeping it a secret from him, do you? (CONOVER *laughs.* MARY *sits on the side of the bed*) Is Grant speaking in Seattle?

CONOVER

Yes, why?

MARY

We were married in Seattle. When I think of Grant speaking there as a candidate for President—

CONOVER

(*Going to her quickly*)

He's not speaking now as a candidate. That's a deep, dark secret. The whole idea of this trip is to create the demand.

MARY

That clears up something you just said—he's your choice first and then the people's choice.

CONOVER

I'm a citizen. I have a right to a choice. I think I've made a good one. And I want to help Grant all I can. He's new at this and needs advice.

MARY

What advice are you giving him?

CONOVER

Oh, so far it's chiefly along the lines of what not to say. Your husband is so afraid of not being completely honest.

MARY

You want him to be honest, don't you?

CONOVER

Oh, yes! (*There is a knock on the door*) Yes? Come in!

(STEVENS *enters.*)

STEVENS

There's a long-distance call for you, sir. It's Wilkes-Barre.

CONOVER

Thank you, Stevens. (*He hesitates for a moment*) I'll take it here. (CONOVER *goes to the telephone.* STEVENS *exits.*)

MARY

Am I in the way?

CONOVER

Not at all. I won't be a minute. (*He picks up the receiver*) Hello. Put him on. (*Pause*) Yes, how are you? (*Pause*) Uh-huh. Yes, Joe, I want the campaign in your district strictly along those lines. If what happens down there is what I think will happen, it'll be a large part of the campaign in '48. How many Italians down there? (*Pause*) What's the size of your Polish vote? (*Pause*) That many? Well, tell them their hope lies in our party. Russia can't be trusted and we'll be tough with her—force her to correct those injustices. (MARY *turns and looks at* CONOVER) You don't have to tell 'em *how*. (MARY *rises, still watching* CONOVER) Go after it, hammer and tongs. You swing that district and we'll get you that veterans' hospital. (*Pause*) Not at all. Good luck. And thanks for calling. (CONOVER *hangs up*) Sorry for the interruption.

MARY

I'm glad it happened. It gave me a chance to change my mind. I'll go with Grant.

CONOVER
(*Heartily*)
That's fine! That pleases me very much. (*He goes to the table and picks up his glass*) That's our first big campaign contribution. To you, my dear, the most attractive plank in your husband's platform.

MARY

That's a hell of a thing to call a woman.

CONOVER
(*Laughing*)
Suppose we go downstairs? I'd like to have you meet the rest of my guests.

MARY

Would it be rude if I postponed that until tomorrow? I have to get a little used to this idea—and I have to get a little used to Grant.

CONOVER

Well, this trip—working along with Grant—by the time you come back you two may be much closer together.

MARY

Even if that could happen, I don't think you'd want it to. It might cost you the support of Mrs. Thorndyke's newspapers.

CONOVER

(*Laughing*)

Don't worry about that. They're Republican newspapers in Republican territory. They couldn't afford to risk their circulation. A chain of newspapers is a very valuable property.

MARY

Mrs. Thorndyke must have thought so. In the divorce settlement Dick Thorndyke got the children and she got the newspapers. And if that sounds bitchy, I hoped it would. You may succeed in killing the rumors, but unfortunately you won't kill Mrs. Thorndyke.

CONOVER

(*Knowingly*)

We may kill more than one rumor.

MARY

Oh, dear! Is there someone I don't know about?

CONOVER

(*With a smile*)

There have been some rumors about you.

MARY

(*Enormously pleased, she walks over to* CONOVER)
There have?

CONOVER

Yes. About you and a certain Major.

MARY

That's wonderful! That's the best news I've had in weeks.
Does Grant know about the Major?

CONOVER

Not so far as I know.

MARY

Well, you're going to tell him, aren't you? I deserve something out of this! I was hoping he'd told *you.*

CONOVER

No, Mrs. Matthews, I have a little intelligence service of
my own.

MARY

Well, it can't be too intelligent. They're considerably be-
hind the times. The Major's been in China for six months.
But when you tell Grant about him, don't let him know the
Major's out of the country.

CONOVER

As far as I'm concerned, the whole thing's a military secret.

MARY

(*Gaily*)

You know, I think I'll go downstairs with you at that! I feel a lot better than I did! Can you wait until I put on a new face? (*She picks up her bag. The door opens and* GRANT *enters. To* GRANT) We were just starting down.

GRANT

You're a little late. The party's breaking up.

CONOVER

We forgot all about you. We've been having a very interesting talk.

GRANT

That puts you one up on me. I've been listening to Governor Dunn. He's just about talked himself to sleep.

CONOVER

I'd better get down there! He doesn't even know where his room is! I'm the night clerk around here. I'll make your excuses, Mrs. Matthews.

MARY

Thanks. Thanks for everything!

CONOVER

Good night. Good night, Grant. (*He starts for the door.*)

GRANT

See you in the morning.

CONOVER

(*At the door*)

Grant, I couldn't wait. I told Mrs. Matthews all about it. (*He gives* GRANT *a reassuring smile and exits quickly.* GRANT *turns and looks at* MARY. *He seems a little uncertain. There is a pause.*)

MARY

Grant, I'm very proud of you.

GRANT

Well, Mary, don't think I'm taking this too seriously.

MARY

I'm taking it seriously. (GRANT *gives her a quick look*) I think it would be a wonderful thing for the country.

GRANT

That's about as nice a thing as you could say, Mary. It's a damn big job. I'm not so sure I've got what it takes.

MARY

Well, I am. It isn't only that you have the brains for it— the important thing to me is—you've always tried to be honest.

GRANT

Tried to be?

MARY

Oh, you've cut some corners in business to get where you wanted to. That's what frightens me a little. But I will say this—you always had the decency to be unhappy about it.

GRANT

(Wryly)

With some help from you.

MARY

But when you weren't thinking of yourself—when it came to what was best for the airplane industry as a whole, I've seen you take some pretty big losses.

GRANT

Right now I'm thinking about the country as a whole. I'm scared, Mary. (*He sits down on the side of the bed.*)

MARY

About being President?

GRANT

No, about what's happening to the country. It's breaking up again . . .

MARY

What do you think you can do about it?

GRANT

I think somebody can appeal to what's best in people instead of what's worst.

MARY

And still be in politics?

GRANT

That's my whole case, Mary. If I can make the people see the choice they've got to make—the choice between their own interests and the interests of the country as a whole—damn it, I think the American people are sound. I think they can be unselfish.

MARY

All of them?

GRANT

Hell, we both know there are plenty of bastards in this world who'll always be out for themselves. But that's where I differ from Conover. I think they're in the minority.

MARY

I do, too. (MARY *sits on the other side of the bed, facing him*) How much do you and Conover differ?

GRANT

He's a politician. Politicians think you have to bribe people to vote for you—one way or another.

MARY

You mean groups like the Poles and the Italians?

GRANT

Yes—and labor and the farmers and the rest of them. But I'm not going to play politics.

MARY

That will take a lot of courage.

GRANT

No, it won't. I have faith in the American people.

MARY

So have I. (*There is a pause*) The Presidency's a great temptation!

GRANT

I don't even want the job. Whether I become President or not is completely unimportant.

(*They look at each other for a moment. Then* MARY *turns away.*)

MARY

Grant, when I first learned the purpose of this trip, I wasn't very happy about making it with you.

GRANT

I can understand that.

MARY

(*Looking back at* GRANT)

But I am now.

GRANT

Mary, there are some things I should say—(*There is a pause, and then he turns away*)—but I can't.

(*The moment is almost too intense.* MARY *stares at* GRANT'S *back for a moment or two, then rises, taking up her hat, gloves and bag from bed.*)

MARY

I think I'll get out of these clothes. (*She exits into the dressing room, leaving the door open.* GRANT *rises and turns to watch the door for a moment. Then* MARY's *voice comes from the dressing room*) Grant!

GRANT

Yes?

MARY

(*Offstage*)

I wish you'd call up Joyce tomorrow.

GRANT

(*Sitting in one of the easy chairs*)

She'll be in school, won't she?

MARY

(*Offstage*)

No, the doctor thinks she shouldn't go back until Wednesday. Oh, she's better. She had no temperature at all today.

GRANT

I'll call around dinner time. Then I can talk to Sonny, too.

MARY

(*Offstage*)

They were both pretty disappointed they couldn't go along.

GRANT

(*Dreamily*)

We ought to be thinking about a good boarding school for those kids.

MARY

(*Offstage*)

For heaven's sake, why?

GRANT

Well, I'm not so sure the White House is a good place to raise children.

MARY

(*Offstage*)

Grant!

GRANT

Yes?

MARY

(*Offstage*)

When are you going to break the news?

GRANT

You mean that I'm a candidate?

MARY

(*Offstage*)

Oh, you're way beyond the nomination—you've elected yourself.

GRANT

(*Grinning*)

I walked into that one—(*Then, defensively*)—but I didn't mean it quite the way it sounded.

MARY

(*Offstage*)

Which one of the plants are we going to first?

GRANT

Minneapolis.

MARY

(*Offstage*)

What are you speaking about there?

GRANT

I'm not making a speech there. That's Stassen territory. Conover thought I might just stir up trouble.

MARY

(*Offstage*)

Uh-huh. I suppose that's good politics. Tell me some more about your differences with Conover.

GRANT

(*Irritated*)

Now wait a minute, Mary! (*He goes to dressing-room door*) That was my decision! I'm making all the decisions! I've told Conover where I stand and he knows I'm going to tell the American people where I stand. (*Starts walking around the room*) The American people are facing problems today that will affect the future of the entire world. There's only one way to face them—with complete honesty—with utter frankness—

MARY
(*Offstage*)

Grant!

GRANT

What?

MARY
(*Offstage*)
Take it easy. I'm going to vote for you.

GRANT

No, I want to straighten you out on this too! If I have anything to offer, it's to change the whole complexion of political
campaigns. I'm not going before the American people telling
them what I can do for them. (MARY *enters in nightgown,
negligee and mules*) But what I *can* do for them is to show
them that the strength of this country, within our own
borders . . .

MARY

Grant! I'm through with the dressing room.

GRANT

I'm in no hurry. (*Resuming his "broadcast"*) The power of
this country, outside our own borders . . .

MARY

Wouldn't you feel more comfortable if you took off that
stuffed shirt?

(GRANT *throws himself down in the chair, sulkily.*)

GRANT

Aw, hell—I don't want to be President.

MARY

(*Going to him*)

Darling, when we were talking a little while ago, you said the same things and they sounded so right—I wish you could just talk to the people that way.

GRANT

(*Not entirely mollified*)

That's the way I plan to talk to them.

MARY

That's all I meant. Got a cigarette? (GRANT *offers her one from his case and lights it for her*) Bill and Amy know we're coming to Seattle? (*She crosses to the bench at foot of bed and sits.*)

GRANT

Bill knows—he expects me at the plant. But they don't know you're coming.

MARY

I'll wire Amy. (*She shakes her head*) Amy—with eight children!

GRANT

Yep, Bill's got the best production record of anyone in the industry.

MARY

I hope Amy's done something about the way she dresses.
She always looks as though somebody bet her she couldn't.

GRANT

(*Laughing*)

Do you remember the way she looked as your bridesmaid?

MARY

No, I was in a complete daze until we got to Victoria.

GRANT

And even in Victoria! When we went into the dining room
you shook hands with the headwaiter! (*They both laugh.
There is an embarrassed pause.* GRANT *straightens up in his
chair, steals a look at* MARY *who is stealing a look at him at
the same time.* GRANT *rises*) Well, I've got a tough day tomorrow. (*He exits into the dressing room, unbuttoning his
coat as he goes and leaving the door open.* MARY *goes back
into her memories for a moment, then throws them off and
starts for her drink on the table. There is a knock on the
door and* MARY *goes to door and opens it.* NORAH *enters with*
MARY's *dress, pressed.*)

NORAH

I was afraid you might have gone to bed. I'll hang it up
for you. (NORAH *starts for the dressing room.*)

MARY

(*Running in front of* NORAH *to dressing-room door*)
My husband's in there!

NORAH

Oh.

GRANT

(*Offstage*)

Did you say something, darling?

MARY

No, dear. It's just the maid with my dress. (*She closes the dressing-room door.* NORAH *drapes the dress carefully over the back of a chair*) What's your name?

NORAH

Norah, Ma'am. (*She takes a blanket from the bed and puts it over the back of chair.*)

MARY

Thank you for pressing it, Norah. I'll hang it up later.

(NORAH *starts preparing the bed, removing the spread and turning back the covers.*)

NORAH

I'm sorry I was so late with it. Just as the iron got hot we got another guest.

MARY

Gracious, where did you put him?

NORAH

He's on a cot in Mr. Conover's room.

MARY

Oh, dear, that makes me feel very guilty.

NORAH

Don't you worry, Mrs. Matthews. A cot's good enough for most of them. They just come down here to get something out of Mr. Conover. Not the people we put in this room. This room is for special guests. We even had a Democrat in this bed one night.

MARY

Oh, I wish you hadn't told me that.

NORAH

He wasn't a Roosevelt Democrat. (NORAH *has finished with the bed and turns on the bed light on table near the bed, then turns to the service-bell cord*) When you wake up in the morning just press this button and I'll have breakfast right up for you.

MARY

Thank you, Norah. Good night.

NORAH

Good night, Ma'am. (*She starts out, then stops and turns*) Oh, I was going to ask your husband but maybe you can tell me. Do you know Mrs. Thorndyke's address?

MARY

Mrs. Thorndyke?

NORAH

She forgot her glasses when she left this morning. And I know what it is to be without glasses. I want to mail them back to her.

MARY

Are you sure they're Mrs. Thorndyke's?

NORAH

(*Getting the glasses from pocket and showing them*)
Yes, they're them Chinese kind. What women won't do! Won't they?

MARY

Yes—won't they? (MARY *places her drink on the desk with considerable emphasis, goes to dressing-room door and opens it, calling in to* GRANT) Grant, can you step out for a minute? Norah wants some information.

GRANT

(*Offstage*)
Be right with you. (MARY *goes to the window and looks out, standing immovable.* GRANT *appears, tying his dressing gown*) Hello, Norah. What can I do for you?

NORAH

Mrs. Thorndyke left her glasses. I wanted to know where to mail them back to her.

GRANT

Oh!—(*He glances toward* MARY)—1276 Park Avenue. Shall I write it down for you?

74

NORAH

No, I can remember it. 1276. 76—that's the year of the revolution, and twelve for the Twelve Commandments.

(NORAH *exits.* GRANT *glances toward* MARY, *who raises the window sharply, her back to him.* GRANT *retreats into the dressing room, closing the door.* MARY *turns, looks after him, studies the bed for a moment and then her eyes go to the overstuffed chairs. She goes into action. She removes three cushions from the overstuffed chairs, placing them in a line on the floor. She then goes to the bed and removes the sheets and blankets. Folding one sheet and one blanket, she makes a bed for one person on one side of the double bed. Then with the other sheet and blanket, she makes a bed on the three cushions on the floor. As she is finishing this,* GRANT *enters from the dressing room in pajamas and dressing gown. He takes in the situation.*)

GRANT

Mary, what do you think you're doing? Now stop that nonsense and make up that bed again. (MARY *finishes fixing the bed on the floor*) Damn it, I'm not going to let you do this! (GRANT *goes to her.* MARY, *ignoring him, takes off her dressing gown, switches off the lights, leaving only the bed lamp burning*) You wouldn't get any sleep down there on the floor and I wouldn't get any sleep lying there worrying about you. (*He points to the double bed.* MARY *crosses quickly to the double bed.*)

MARY

Good night, Mr. President! (*She pops into the double bed, turning off the bed lamp.* GRANT *looks at the bed on the floor with dismay as the curtain falls.*)

ACT TWO

ACT TWO

The living room of a suite at the Book-Cadillac Hotel in Detroit. It is furnished the way a living room in the Book-Cadillac Hotel would be furnished—in fact the Book-Cadillac has furnished it for us—a desk, a telephone, a sofa, several easy chairs, and a highboy. The pictures on the wall are surprisingly enough not French prints but modern paintings.

The entrance from the hall is upstage, center. Down right and down left are the two doors leading into the bedrooms of the suite.

At rise the stage is dark; then the door to the hall opens and a BELLBOY *enters, puts down three bags he is carrying and switches on the lights.*

MARY *and* GRANT *follow him, arm-in-arm.* GRANT *is carrying a handful of telegrams, some of them already opened.*

BELLBOY

Well, we made it.

GRANT

Thanks! That was slick. We'd have never got through that crowd in the lobby.

BELLBOY

Remember that if you get trapped again. The service elevators are right back of the passenger elevators.

MARY

It was exciting, wasn't it? At the station, too. What a mob!

GRANT

I thought Spike would meet us. I guess he didn't get my telegram.

MARY

Just the same I'm glad he came on ahead. This is more like it.

BELLBOY

Where shall I put the bags?

GRANT

Mary, pick a room for yourself, will you? (GRANT *throws his coat and hat on a chair, goes to the desk, puts down the telegrams, and picks up the telephone.* MARY *opens the door of the bedroom to the left and looks in*) Hello, what room is Mr. MacManus in?

MARY

That's a nice room. (*She crosses to the right bedroom.*)

GRANT
(*Into the telephone*)

What? (*Pause*) E. J. MacManus. (*Pause*) Ring it, will you?

MARY
(*Looking into the right bedroom*)

One room's as good as another. (*She turns to the* BELLBOY) Where are Mr. Matthews' bags?

BELLBOY

I'll bring them right up.

MARY

Well, you can put those in here. (*She exits into the right bedroom followed by* BELLBOY *with her bags.*)

GRANT

(*Into the telephone*)

Hello, Spike. (*Pause*) Just this minute. We were grounded in Springfield. Come on up. We're in 2519. (*Pause*) Jim? The hell he is! Telephone the desk and tell them when he gets here to send him right up to the suite. (*Pause*) We're having a drink. What will you have, an old-fashioned? (*Pause*) Right. I'll order a drink for Jim too. Come on up. (*He clicks the receiver, staying on the phone*) Room service. (*Pause*) Room service? This is 2519. Will you send up two martinis— (MARY *enters from the right bedroom*)—one old-fashioned, and a Scotch and soda right away? Thanks.

MARY

Who are all the drinks for?

GRANT

Spike and Jim.

MARY

Is Conover here?

GRANT

He's on his way up from the station. That's a good sign, Mary. It looks as though Jim's afraid somebody might get his front seat on the bandwagon. (GRANT *has started opening the telegrams*) Here! Let's get to work on these telegrams. (*He hands* MARY *some of the wires, then goes left to sofa and sits.*)

MARY

I'm not so sure that's the reason Jim came out here.

GRANT
(*Absorbed in the telegrams*)
Yeah?

MARY
(*Going to him*)
Grant, don't talk to Jim about what you're going to say tonight.

GRANT
(*Excitedly*)
These wires are all about the Wichita speech. They're terrific. I've never had anything like this before.

MARY

That's what I mean. Spike tried to talk you out of making that speech. So remember what I just said.

GRANT
(*Looking up*)
What'd you just say?

MARY

Don't talk to Jim about your speech tonight.

GRANT

O.K. Mary, listen to this one. . . .

(*The* BELLBOY *enters from the right bedroom.*)

BELLBOY

I turned on the radiator and opened the windows. You've got plenty of towels. Is there anything else I can do?

MARY

Yes, you can get the other bags.

BELLBOY

Oh, yes. Coming right up. (*The* BELLBOY *exits.*)

MARY

(*Glancing through the telegrams*)

Grant—these are simply wonderful! You see, you didn't have to be afraid of shooting the works. That's the way they want to hear you talk.

GRANT

Just look at these, Mary—it shows how hungry the American people are for leadership.

MARY

This one's nice, Grant. It mentions your modesty and humility.

GRANT

Well, here's one who didn't like it.

MARY

Who's that?

GRANT

I don't know. Executive Secretary, Local 801. . . . (*He crumples the telegram and throws it away.*)

MARY

Look, darling—they want you to speak in Omaha next Monday.

GRANT

That's nothing. They want me in New Orleans on Thursday and Atlanta on Friday.

MARY

Let's go—(*She sits on the sofa beside him*)—let's go to all three of them!

GRANT

Mary, Omaha is way back there—(*He gestures*)—New Orleans and Atlanta are way down there—(*He gestures*)—New York is over there—(*Another gesture*)—and the work on my desk is up to here. (*He indicates his chin.*)

MARY

I don't know why you bother with business when this is so much fun.

(*They grin at each other.*)

GRANT

Do you know, this trip has done you a lot of good? You have no right to look that young at your age! On the field at Denver, just before we took off, I had the damnedest sensation. You were standing there in the moonlight with the wind from the propeller blowing your hair and your dress— I knew we were in Denver, but you were the girl standing on the deck of the boat on our way to Victoria.

MARY

(*After a reminiscent pause*)

Now I'll tell you something. Remember in Victoria when we stood on the balcony of the hotel and you were telling me what the world should be like? That same boy was standing on the platform last night in Wichita.

GRANT

I'm glad you said that, Mary. It was a wonderful satisfaction, that speech—just saying what I really believed.

MARY

(*She holds up the telegrams*)

You see what that speech did! (*She looks down at the top telegram*) Grant, who's Herbert Bayard Swope?

(*There is a knock on the door.*)

GRANT

Come in! (SPIKE *enters, carrying the Detroit newspapers.* MARY *and* GRANT *rise and greet him*) Hello, Spike.

SPIKE

Hi-ya.

85

MARY

Hello, Spike, we finally got here.

SPIKE

You had me worried. You jammed up a lot of appointments when your plane was grounded.

MARY

Don't tell Grant I said so—but there's nothing like a train.

GRANT

Those the evening papers? (*He takes the papers from* SPIKE *and starts reading them*) Hmm! Front-page spread!

SPIKE

Did the newspaper boys get you at the station?

GRANT

(*Sitting in chair left*)
Yeah—a flock of them. (*He is still reading paper*) Mary! (*In the play* GRANT *reads a headline that would be in a Detroit newspaper the night of the performance. This headline is changed every night*) Jim's coming out here makes things look pretty hot.

MARY

Is he staying here?

SPIKE

Yes, damn it—and I have to split my bed with him. You know what kind of split a politician takes.

86

MARY

That's silly. We have two bedrooms here and we don't need both of them. Grant, you're moving in with me. We're putting Jim in the other bedroom. (GRANT *is absorbed in the* *paper*) Grant! Yoo-hoo! Mr. Candidate! Mr. President!

GRANT

(*Looking up*)

Huh?

MARY

That got him! (*To* GRANT) I'm playing a little politics for you. I'm saving Jim from sleeping with Spike. We're putting him in our extra bedroom.

GRANT

Fine! Be with you in a minute, Spike. Let me finish this editorial.

(*There is a knock on the door.*)

SPIKE

I've got some people coming to see you but they're not due this early. (SPIKE *goes to the door and opens it.* CONOVER *enters*) Hello, Jim!

CONOVER

Hello, Spike. (*He greets* MARY) Mary!

MARY

So nice seeing you, Jim. We didn't expect you. (*She offers him her cheek, which he kisses.* GRANT *rises.*)

CONOVER

(*Going to* GRANT *and shaking hands*)

Hello, Grant! Politics agrees with you—you're looking fine.

GRANT

I feel great. Look, headlines and a damn good editorial! It's about the Wichita speech—the responsibility of the labor unions. Says it's about time somebody brought it out into the open.

MARY

Jim, it was the best speech Grant ever made. It was the first time I felt sure he could be elected. You never heard such applause.

CONOVER

Mary, if applause elected Presidents, William Jennings Bryan would have had three terms.

GRANT

It's good to see you.

MARY

We're putting you in our other bedroom.

CONOVER

Fine! My bags are down in the lobby.

GRANT

What news have you brought us? I'm certainly glad you're here.

MARY

Yes, it will give you a chance to see Grant in front of an audience.

CONOVER

Oh, I'm not making any public appearances. I'm not supposed to be in Detroit. Don't let anyone know I'm in town. I thought I should come out and bring you up to date on things and go over the situation. What are you talking about here tonight?

GRANT

Well, it's the last speech of the tour, Jim. It's got a little bit of everything.

CONOVER

Anything controversial?

MARY

Not for anybody that agrees with him. I want you to see these telegrams. (MARY *goes to the desk*.)

SPIKE

They got here three hours late. (*To* GRANT) I was pretty sure you'd make the broadcast. You don't go on until after the banquet.

MARY

Is this another banquet?

SPIKE

Yeah.

MARY

Then we'd better have dinner before we go. (MARY *picks up the telephone and speaks into it*) Room service, please. What do you want to eat, Grant?

(SPIKE *takes the telegrams from* MARY *and hands them to* CONOVER *who glances at them casually*.)

GRANT

Anything that's ready—hamburger if they've got it.

SPIKE

I won't have time to eat with you. Better make it snappy. You're going to be busy.

MARY

Jim, what shall I order for you?

CONOVER

I'll have some chicken—and some coffee.

MARY

You can't have chicken and eat with us. I never want to see another chicken.

GRANT

Every time we sit down in a chair, somebody puts chicken in front of us. (*He pulls up a trouser-leg and points to his calf*) Look—pin-feathers!

CONOVER

All right. I'll have hamburger too—hamburger and onions.

MARY

(*Into the telephone*)

Room service? (*Pause*) This is room— (*She looks inquiringly toward the men.*)

SPIKE

2519.

MARY

2519. Have you any hamburger? (*Pause*) That's fine. Three hamburger steaks, one with onions—two without, damn it, and whatever goes with it—except spinach. (*To the men*) Anybody want dessert? Ice cream's always safe.

GRANT

Fine!

CONOVER

None for me.

MARY

(*Into the telephone*)

One chocolate ice cream. And three coffees. Will you hurry it, please? (*She hangs up. There is a knock on the door*) Come in! (*The* BELLBOY *enters with* GRANT's *bags. He is followed by* WAITER *with a tray of drinks. To the* BELLBOY) Put all the bags in there. (*She indicates the right bedroom. She takes a cocktail from the tray*) We ordered a highball for you, Jim.

91

CONOVER

Thanks.

(*The* WAITER *serves the others their drinks.*)

SPIKE

Are you the floor waiter?

WAITER

Yes, sir.

SPIKE

There's a dinner order in. Hurry it up for us, will you?
(*To* GRANT) I've got a lot of people lined up for you to see.

GRANT

Can't I see them after the banquet?

SPIKE

You were supposed to see them this afternoon, but you
didn't get in, so I bunched them all between seven and
seven-thirty.

CONOVER

Well, I can't have dinner here if a lot of people are coming
in.

SPIKE

No, it's O.K. I can keep this room clear. I'll juggle the
visiting firemen between the two bedrooms. Grant can duck
in and say hello, and come back and eat. We'll clear them
all up in a hurry.

(*The* BELLBOY *enters from the right bedroom.*)

BELLBOY

I've turned off the radiator and closed the windows. Anything else I can do?

GRANT

No, thanks. (GRANT *tips the* BELLBOY, *who exits. The* WAITER *goes to* GRANT *who takes the check and writes on it.*)

CONOVER

Are you touching on labor again tonight?

GRANT

No!

MARY

(*Cutting in quickly*)

Grant, we won't have time to dress after dinner. We ought to be changing now.

GRANT

Yes, we can be changed by the time dinner gets here.

(*The* WAITER *starts out and* MARY *stops him.*)

MARY

Waiter! Another drink, Jim?

CONOVER

No, thanks.

MARY

Spike?

SPIKE

Not now.

MARY

How about you, Grant? Another cocktail while you're dressing?

GRANT

I don't dare. I've got to make a speech.

MARY

(*To the* WAITER)

Bring another martini to the bedroom.

WAITER

Right away, Ma'am. (*The* WAITER *exits.*)

MARY

(*Moving toward the right bedroom*)

That's the difference between Grant and me—I'd rather be tight than be President. (MARY *exits.*)

GRANT

Spike, we haven't opened all those telegrams. Look through them, will you? (GRANT *starts to exit.*)

CONOVER

Grant, while you're dressing, have you got a copy of your speech tonight that I could be glancing at?

GRANT

(*At the bedroom door*)

It's not a set speech, Jim. I'm talking from notes.

94

CONOVER

Could I be looking over the notes?

GRANT

They're just some memos I scribbled down—I'm sorry, Jim, they wouldn't mean a thing to you. (SPIKE *has picked up the telegrams*) I'll tell you what you can read. Spike, show him some more of my fan mail. (GRANT *exits into the right bedroom.* SPIKE *turns to look at* CONOVER.)

CONOVER

(*Angrily*)

You're a hell of a campaign manager!

SPIKE

(*On the defensive*)

That's why I wired for you, Jim. He's gotten away from me.

CONOVER

It's a damn shame! The boys in the Northwest and all along the Coast—they were swinging right in behind him. Then he had to stick out his chin in Wichita.

SPIKE

How much damage has he done?

CONOVER

We may have lost labor. I must have had thirty calls after that speech. How did you let it happen?

SPIKE

I talked him out of that labor stuff in Denver—that is, I gave him something to use instead—local stuff—Rocky Mountain stuff.

CONOVER

Didn't you get a look at the speech for Wichita?

SPIKE

No, and I'll tell you why. She—(*He points to the right bedroom*)—knew he was planning to talk about labor in Denver and when he didn't she spent the rest of the night tossing harpoons into him. But the next day on the plane to Wichita they were clubby as hell—and I couldn't get any advance copy of the speech. You just sent the wrong dame with him!

CONOVER

I even talked him into taking her along.

SPIKE

When we get back to New York, Kay can straighten him out. She put this Presidential bee in his bonnet. She never tears Grant down. She always builds him up. If you ask me, that's why he fell for her. But that doesn't help us tonight.

CONOVER

What are you afraid of tonight?

SPIKE

I don't know—(*The telephone rings*)—but she's too damn happy. (SPIKE *answers the telephone*) Hello. (*Pause*) Oh—

96

give me the desk. (*To* CONOVER) That's why I sent for you. We can't take a chance on his making another mistake here tonight. (*Into the telephone*) Hello. This is MacManus. There are some people down there to see Mr. Matthews. And there are a lot more coming. Send them all up to the twenty-fifth floor, Parlor B, and tell them to wait for me there. (*He hangs up. Then speaks to* CONOVER) You've got to find out what he's talking about here. (SPIKE *picks up telegrams and joins* CONOVER *on the sofa.*)

CONOVER

That's what I was trying to do—and you saw how far I got. (CONOVER *glances through some of the telegrams, then tosses them aside.*)

SPIKE

Well, keep after him.

CONOVER

If you've got people coming to see him, what chance have I?

SPIKE

I wasn't sure you were going to get here. I figured I had to put some kind of pressure on him. I've got everybody— dairy farmers, automobile people, even the labor boys, mad as they are.

CONOVER

Maybe they ought to be talking to Mrs. Matthews.

SPIKE

Look, Jim, this guy's vulnerable. He's got the bug.

CONOVER

That's what I was counting on. How bad has he got it?

SPIKE

He wants to be President, all right. So what I keep throwing at him is votes—get those votes—don't lose those votes. (CONOVER *rises*. SPIKE *looks up from the telegrams he has been reading*) Say, maybe that Wichita speech didn't do as much harm as we thought it did.

CONOVER

Oh, those are just from people.

SPIKE

They don't count, eh?

CONOVER

You don't see any signed "State Chairman," do you?

SPIKE

Don't kid yourself, this guy does something to people. I've been on a lot of campaigns. They don't shake hands with Grant just to say they've shaken hands with him. They're up there with a light in their eyes—they practically mob him. If he gets away from us, you may be heading a "Stop Matthews" movement.

CONOVER

Stopping him wouldn't be any trouble. He hasn't any or-

ganization. I don't want to stop him. I think we can elect
him, if we can keep him in line.

(SPIKE *is studying another telegram.*)

SPIKE

Say, Jim, did you arrange this?

CONOVER

What?

SPIKE

He's speaking in New York—the 23rd—Foreign Policy
Association.

CONOVER

The hell he is! Why doesn't he consult us?

SPIKE

He didn't even mention it to me. Just because I don't trust
him doesn't mean he shouldn't trust me.

CONOVER

That forces us right out into the open. What's that date?

SPIKE

The twenty-third.

CONOVER

He can't speak there and pretend he's not a candidate. Besides that, he's got to go along with us on foreign policy. Our

big chance to win is with the foreign vote. Well, I guess we've got to fence him in. Damn!

SPIKE

He wants that nomination. He wants to be President.

CONOVER

Then I'd better face him with some people who can deliver delegates—people he knows he has to have to win—I'd like to throw them at him all at once.

SPIKE

Better line up a big shot from labor.

CONOVER

Yes—Bill Hardy would do that for me. I could get Senator Lauterback to scare hell out of him on the farm vote.

SPIKE

You'd better have Kay there. I know damn well he listens to her.

CONOVER

Who would talk for business? Look around at the banquet tonight, Spike, and see if there's anybody who could be useful.

(*There is a knock at the door.*)

SPIKE

Damn it. I told them to send everybody to Parlor B. (*He goes to door and opens it. It is the* WAITER.)

WAITER

I have the dinner—and the extra cocktail.

SPIKE

Wheel it in!

(*The* WAITER *wheels in a table with service for three and* MARY's *second cocktail.* SPIKE *goes to the bedroom door and knocks.*)

GRANT
(*Offstage*)

Yes?

SPIKE

Dinner's here.

GRANT
(*Offstuge*)

We'll be right out.

SPIKE

Does Mary want her other cocktail in there?

MARY
(*Offstage*)

Cocktails don't have to come to me. I come to them. (MARY *enters in a dinner dress. The* WAITER *serves* MARY *the cocktail.*)

WAITER

I have the dinner right outside. (*He exits and returns immediately with portable oven. During the following scene, he sets the table and puts three chairs in their proper places.*)

SPIKE

(*Going to the bedroom door*)

Grant, is your room free?

GRANT

(*Offstage*)

All set. I'm just tying my tie.

SPIKE

When you're through, will you unlock the hall door to your room?

GRANT

(*Offstage*)

Okay.

MARY

(*To the* WAITER)

Serve it as soon as you're ready.

SPIKE

(*Hurriedly going to the other bedroom*)

I'd better unlock the hall door to this one, too. (SPIKE *exits into left bedroom.*)

CONOVER

(*To* MARY)

My dear, that's a little unfair.

MARY

What?

CONOVER

I'm afraid that instead of listening to Grant they'll be just looking at you tonight.

MARY

Thank you, Jim. I'm so willing to believe that, I'm going to pretend you're not a politician.

(SPIKE *returns from the left bedroom.*)

SPIKE

All right. Here we go. I'll bring in the first batch of patriots. (*To* MARY) Remind Grant they've got votes.

MARY

Spike does take the nobility out of a crusade.

SPIKE

(*At the hall doorway*)

Am I expected to be noble? On my salary! (*He exits into the hall.*)

CONOVER

Why don't you just spend the evening here with me? You've probably read Grant's speech anyway, haven't you?

MARY

I'm sorry you won't be there.

CONOVER

I'll listen to it on the radio—if I can get a radio—and if I can't—what's he speaking about?

MARY

Oh, I think we can get you a radio. (*She goes to the telephone.* GRANT *enters from the right bedroom.*)

GRANT

I damn near left these notes in my other suit. (*He starts looking through some notes he has in his hand.*)

MARY

(*Into the telephone*)

Could you have a radio sent up to 2519 right away? (*Pause*) It's very important. (*Pause*) Thank you! (*She hangs up*) It looks as though you'll have to listen, Jim. They think you can have one.

CONOVER

(*To* GRANT)

If you want to rehearse any of that, Grant, I'll be glad to have you try it out on me.

GRANT

I'll give you the start— (*He speaks as though he were addressing a large auditorium*) Ladies—and members of the Automotive Council of Detroit. I know that I am among friends here tonight—and it would be unfriendly of me not to talk to you with utter frankness and naked honesty. In the economic anarchy we are facing today—

(*The* WAITER *has taken two plates of food out of the portable oven.*)

104

WAITER

Who's with onions?

CONOVER

(*Sourly*)

I'm with onions.

(MARY *goes to the center place at the table and sits. The two men go to either side and sit. The* WAITER *serves them.*)

WAITER

Watch the plates—they're very hot.

GRANT

Looks good—I can hardly wait. Waiter, you've got a starving man on your hands.

WAITER

Watch the plate. I'll bring the dessert in fifteen minutes. (*The* WAITER *exits, with the portable oven.*)

GRANT

Ah—meat! And can I use it? (*He has his knife and fork poised when* SPIKE *enters from the right bedroom.*)

SPIKE

Grant, your public is waiting.

GRANT

My hamburger's waiting.

SPIKE

Hamburgers don't vote. These are dairy farmers. (*He goes to* GRANT *and hands him a slip of paper, pointing to a name at the top*) The fellow with the mustache is the one to play for.

GRANT

Just the Number Five handshake, Spike?

SPIKE

No, a little talk. You know—cows, butter, milk, cheese—since the war American cheese has become big industry.

GRANT

What do I know about American cheese?

SPIKE

Walk this way and meet three perfect specimens. (GRANT *rises and starts out*) Remember— (GRANT *turns*) They mean votes! (GRANT *exits into the right bedroom*) Well—now I'll set 'em up in the other alley. (*He exits into the hall.*)

MARY

(*Eagerly*)

How do you think Grant's doing? What are your reports?

CONOVER

First let me tell you about my reports on you. You've done a great job, and I want to congratulate you.

MARY

Well, I'd like to admit something if I could be sure it wouldn't be used against me. I've enjoyed it—every minute of it.

CONOVER

Even the speeches?

MARY

That's been the best part of it. I don't mean just listening to Grant. I mean listening to the people—feeling the way they respond. Of course they laugh and yell when he talks about the troubles he's had getting things through in Washington . . .

CONOVER

(*Busily eating*)

Yes, I've heard those laughs. He does it very cleverly. That's what they like to hear.

MARY

Jim, over the radio you only hear the audience when it's making noise. What you don't hear is the silence—when Grant has them so that they're not thinking of themselves—when he has them thinking of the country—that's when it takes your breath away.

CONOVER

I'm glad to hear Grant can do that. I know how effective it can be in a speaker.

MARY

Jim, I'm not talking about Grant. When they rush up after the speeches—I wish you could see their faces. You know, I'd forgotten how good it was to be with people—I used to see a lot of them when Grant first started and had small plants—when we moved to New York I got too far away from them—They're so eager to do whatever is the best thing to do—and they're so quick—they're so intelligent. (*She laughs*) They've thrown a couple of questions at Grant that had him stopped cold. He just had to admit he didn't know enough to answer them. And they liked him for it.

CONOVER

That's smart. Shows he uses his head.

MARY

(*Sitting back in her chair and regarding* CONOVER *quizzically*)

Jim, you fascinate me. You have such a complete lack of faith in sincerity—and you're so sincere about it. (CONOVER *gives her an understanding smile*) What puzzles me is that I dislike so thoroughly the way your mind works—and yet I'm so very fond of you.

CONOVER

It is puzzling, isn't it, because I feel the same way toward you.

(*She pats his hand with fond reproof.*)

108

MARY

You're so cynical.

(CONOVER *pats her hand in same manner.*)

CONOVER

You're so unrealistic.

(*They grin at each other.* GRANT *enters from the right bedroom.*)

MARY

(*To* GRANT)

Well, how's the farmer's choice?

GRANT

(*Going to the table*)

After the beautiful things I have just said about cows, I shouldn't touch this hamburger. It's like eating an old friend. But I'm going to. (*He sits down and gets ready to eat the hamburger.* SPIKE *enters from the left bedroom.*)

SPIKE

Ah, back from the pastures. Wipe off your feet and come in and meet the A. F. of L.

GRANT

Look, Spike, give me a chance to eat . . .

SPIKE

Nope. This is a crisis. I have to know you're holding the

A. F. of L. in there while I sneak the C.I.O into the other bedroom.

> GRANT

Put them both in the same room, I'll talk to them both at the same time.

> SPIKE

Little Boy Blue, haven't you heard? They ain't keeping steady company any more. Besides these aren't big shots—just small fry—officers in the locals.

> GRANT

They're both labor groups. They both want the same thing. That's what I've been talking about all this time—getting people to work together—now let's put it into action.

> SPIKE .

Now, boss . . .

> GRANT

I'm serious about this, Spike. Tell those men in there you're bringing in the C.I.O., and then I'll come in and talk to them!

> (SPIKE *shrugs and exits into the left bedroom.* MARY *preens herself, looking proudly from* GRANT *to* CONOVER.)

> CONOVER

Grant, aren't you just asking for trouble?

> GRANT

Jim, I've got both organizations working in my plants. I can walk into a recreation room where C.I.O. and A. F. of L.

men are there together and talk to them—talk labor to them. Bill Green and Phil Murray will both sit down with each other. The big boys in labor are all right, except for Lewis. (*He points to the left bedroom*) This is the type of men we've got to get together.

CONOVER

I don't mind your having your head in the clouds—but I wish you'd keep your feet in the voting booth.

GRANT

Jim, if I can ever make people like these in the next room see something bigger than their job as head of their own locals and the little power they get from that . . .

MARY

(*To* CONOVER)

There may be some votes in that, too.

CONOVER

One of the things I came down to talk to you about—I got a very bad reaction to your speech in Wichita.

GRANT

Did you read those telegrams?

CONOVER

You may have picked up a few votes there in the auditorium, but you've chilled off most of the labor leaders in the country. I know! I've talked to them!

GRANT

I said that business had to give labor a voice in management. That didn't chill them off, did it?

CONOVER

No, no, that was all right—for labor.

GRANT

I said that labor had to have a fairer share of the profits. Did they object to that?

CONOVER

No, damn it—it was the stand you took on strikes.

GRANT

(*Earnestly*)

No, Jim, not on strikes. I mentioned only one kind of strike. I asked labor to give the people of this country the answer to this question: "Is there any moral justification for the jurisdictional strike?" Can you answer that question? Can the labor leaders you talked to answer that question?

CONOVER

Of course they can't. That's what makes them so sore. Too bad you didn't talk about the other kind of strikes.

GRANT

All right, it's true—some unions are abusing their right to strike at this time. They're sacrificing the country for their own special interest. What do you propose to do? Take their right to strike away from them? Freedom of the press is being abused. Do you want to take that right away from publishers?

CONOVER

(*Grudgingly*)

Well—labor's pretty sore about what you said about opening their books, too.

GRANT

Not all of them are. Some of the biggest and best unions in the country have opened their books.

MARY

Jim, the audience was full of union men—I don't mean union leaders, I mean union members—and they cheered Grant. I had a feeling they'd like to get a look at those books themselves.

CONOVER

Some of that money goes into campaign contributions.

(SPIKE *enters from the left bedroom.*)

GRANT

Well?

SPIKE

No dice. They're even mad they're in the same hotel together.

GRANT

That makes me pretty mad, too.

SPIKE

Boss, you've got to speak to them.

GRANT

(*He throws down napkin and rises*)
Of course I'll speak to them. How am I going to do what
I want to do if I don't speak to them?

SPIKE

Here are the names. (*He hands* GRANT *a slip of paper*)
Watch out for the little guy they call Mac. (GRANT *angrily
grabs the paper, and exits into the left bedroom*) Now for
some counter-espionage. (SPIKE *exits into the hall.*)

MARY

(*Earnestly*)
Jim, Grant's got something. Don't take it away from him!
When he's just cockeyed drunk with sincerity people can't
resist him!

CONOVER

That statement sounds as though it includes you, too.

MARY

Let me straighten you out about Grant and me. Our personal relations are strictly political.

CONOVER

I thought I saw Grant throw a look or two at you tonight
that wasn't entirely impersonal.

MARY

Jim, you're a bachelor, aren't you?

CONOVER

Theoretically. Why?

MARY

It's just that if you'd been married, you'd understand.

CONOVER

Understand what?

MARY

When a man and woman have been married for a long time even their closest friends can't always tell whether they're still in love with each other. They themselves wonder about it sometimes.

CONOVER

Well, then the trip's accomplished something—if you're at the point of wondering.

MARY

No, there are things that happen that make you sure—little things that don't really mean anything except that you know how much they do mean. For instance, Grant found out once the girls at school used to call me Maizie. He knew I hated it. So sometimes he used to call me Maizie—just to tease me —but you don't tease people that way unless you love each other. Well, Maizie doesn't live here any more. And another thing—Grant always hated to hear me swear—whenever I

let go with something—he used to smack me on the behind—
hard. I've done a lot of swearing on this trip—

CONOVER

And no smacks?

MARY

(*Wistfully*)

It's a small request—but I'd give anything for a good smack
on the behind.

CONOVER

I wish there were something I could do about that.

(SPIKE *enters from the right bedroom.*)

SPIKE

Still in with them?

MARY

Yes, and all's quiet on the Western front.

SPIKE

Well, the Eastern front is ready.

(GRANT *enters from the left bedroom, closing the door
behind him.*)

GRANT

(*To* SPIKE)

Are the C.I.O. boys in there?

SPIKE

Yes—and in what I would call an ugly mood.

GRANT

Keep your back turned, Jim. (GRANT *opens the left bedroom door*) This way, gentlemen. (*Three stony-faced labor leaders march in from the left bedroom, and* GRANT *leads them toward the right bedroom.* MARY *springs up to greet them. As each one is introduced, they shake hands with* MARY, *then continue into the right bedroom*) This is Mrs. Matthews! Mr. Vincent.

MARY

How do you do?

GRANT

Mr. Solly.

MARY

How do you do?

GRANT

Mr. Mack.

MARY

How do you do?

GRANT

Right in here, gentlemen. (*He opens the right bedroom door and they file in.* GRANT *turns and gives a broad wink to* MARY *and* CONOVER *and follows in after them, closing the door.* SPIKE *puts his fingers in his ears and stands shuddering as though he expects an explosion behind him, then relaxes with a grin.*)

SPIKE

You know, Grant might be able to unite the United Nations. (*He starts out, sees* GRANT's *food, walks to* GRANT's *place, sits and picks up the knife and fork.*)

117

MARY

Spike, don't you dare touch that!

(SPIKE *rises*.)

SPIKE

All right, I can starve. But that's the way you make Communists. (*He exits into the hall.*)

MARY

Poor Grant. He's not getting a thing to eat. (*She goes to the desk and gets a cigarette from her evening bag and lights it.*)

CONOVER

I was hoping we three could have a quiet dinner together and talk.

MARY

We'll see you after we get back here.

CONOVER

I'd like to go over with Grant what he's speaking about tonight. Tell me something about it.

MARY

Well, it's his last speech of the trip. It's sort of a summary.

CONOVER

Detroit's a dangerous city politically—almost anything you say here is controversial.

MARY

Isn't a Presidential campaign supposed to be controversial?

CONOVER

Yes, but they've had a lot of trouble here—strikes—race riots—and for some reason or other it seems to be the headquarters of the lunatic fringe.

MARY

You mean the subversive groups . . .

CONOVER

Mary, subversive is a very dangerous word— (*Apprehensively*) Grant's not using that word in his speech tonight, is he?

MARY

I think Grant's saving anything like that—and the international situation—for his speech in New York.

CONOVER

Oh, is he speaking in New York?

MARY

Yes! (GRANT *enters from the right bedroom*) Still alive?

GRANT

Yes, and so are they. (*He goes to the table*) As a matter of fact, the Congress of Industrial Organizations has just extended an invitation to the American Federation of Labor to have a glass of beer.

CONOVER
(With a bit of a grin)
Under whose jurisdiction?

GRANT
The Arcade Bar and Grill! (*He starts to eat.*)

CONOVER
Mary tells me you're making a speech in New York.

GRANT
(Gratified)
Yes. The twenty-third. Foreign Policy Association! That's moving into the big time!

CONOVER
You couldn't postpone that, could you? I don't see how you can open up on the international situation and still pretend you're not a candidate.

GRANT
I didn't think I could turn it down.

CONOVER
Well, it's too late, I guess. (*Disturbed*) I couldn't very well advise you about something I didn't know anything about.

(SPIKE *enters from the left bedroom.*)

SPIKE

Okay, Grant, if you're ready!

GRANT

(*Starting to eat again*)

Spike, they can't be more important than this hamburger.

SPIKE

Well, they're all your friends. It's the Detroit tycoon set.

GRANT

(*Rising with alacrity*)

Oh, somebody I really want to see? You're slipping, Spike. (*He exits into the left bedroom.*)

SPIKE

I've got one more set. They're gate crashers. Even I don't know who they are. (SPIKE *exits into the hall.*)

MARY

(*Putting out her cigarette*)

I wonder whether I have time to sneak a look in a mirror? (*She starts for the right bedroom, then stops.* CONOVER *rises*) Oh, I forgot to thank you for telling Grant the gossip about me.

CONOVER

I didn't tell him.

MARY

Well, somebody must have told him.

CONOVER

Has he said anything?

MARY

No, but he's very rude to all army Majors. (CONOVER *chuckles*) And it's so unfair to those poor Majors. My Major's been a Colonel for months.

CONOVER

I hadn't heard about that.

MARY

Jim, your secret service works backwards. They keep secrets from you!

(GRANT *enters from the left bedroom.*)

GRANT

Mary, Sam Parrish is in here. He'd like to say hello to you.

MARY

Good! I haven't seen Sam for ages.

CONOVER

Wait, Mary! Grant, I'd like to have a few words with Parrish myself. Could you have him step in here?

GRANT

Sure, I'll tell him.

CONOVER

Oh, Grant—don't let the others know I'm here.

(GRANT *exits into the left bedroom.* CONOVER *moves up out of range of door, pulling his chair with him.*)

MARY

We've known Sam for years. We're very fond of him.

CONOVER

So am I. He's raised a lot of money for the party.

(SAM PARRISH *enters from the left bedroom. He is the successful American business man and looks it. He sees* MARY *and goes to her.*)

SAM

Hello, Mary! You're a sight for sore eyes! (*He kisses her.*)

MARY

Hello, Sam!

SAM

Mary, I'll be in New York for our annual dinner on the seventeenth. This time it's on me!

MARY

No, Sam, you're having dinner with us.

SAM

My, you're just as pretty as you ever were! I could eat you with a spoon. . . . (*He swings* MARY *around exuberantly and catches sight of* CONOVER) Why, Jim Conover, you old son-of-a-gun!

CONOVER

Hi-ya, Sam!

SAM

What are you doing here?

CONOVER

Take it easy, Sam. You're the only one in Detroit who knows I am here—and keep it to yourself!

SAM

What the hell's going on? Say— (*He looks from* CONOVER *to* MARY *and then the dawn breaks*) Damn it, I might have known! Jim, do you know you're psychic? I'm due in Washington on the eighteenth—I had it all planned to come and see you with the idea of selling you Grant Matthews for President, and damn it you beat me to it. Frankly, I was going to bribe you—with the biggest campaign contribution you ever saw.

CONOVER

(*Grabbing* SAM's *hand and shaking it*)

That's a date, Sam! Lunch in Washington on the eighteenth and bring cash!

SAM

(*Gleefully*)

Mary, you go right home and start packing. You're moving into the White House. Give me another kiss! (*He kisses her again*) I've never been so happy about anything in my life. Wait until I tell Hilda!

CONOVER

Sam, you're not telling anybody, including Hilda.

MARY

How is Hilda? Is she coming to the banquet?

SAM

No, damn it, she's in bed with the flu. She's so mad she's going to miss Grant's speech she's not fit to live with. Look— why don't you call her up? Niagara 2956.

MARY

I'd better call her now because I'm not sure you and Hilda will be speaking to us after Grant's speech tonight. (MARY *goes to the telephone and picks up the receiver.*)

CONOVER
(*To* MARY, *sharply*)

Why do you say that?

SAM
(*To* CONOVER)

The last time I was in New York, Grant and I had a hell of a knockdown drag-out fight about reconversion and full employment.

CONOVER

(*To* MARY)

Mary, is that what Grant's talking about tonight?

MARY

(*Into the telephone*)

Just a minute. (*To* SAM) What's that number again, Sam?

SAM

Niagara 2956.

MARY

(*Into the telephone*)

Niagara 2956.

SAM

(*To* CONOVER)

You know Grant—likes to talk like a radical, but, hell, anybody that's made as much money as Grant has is a sound American.

(GRANT *enters from the left bedroom.*)

GRANT

The other boys thought they ought to hurry over there, Sam. Why don't you stick around a while and go over with us?

SAM

No, I've got to go with them. I'm chairman of the committee.

GRANT

You can catch them at the elevator. I'll let you out this way. (*He takes* SAM *to the hall door.*)

SAM

I'll come back after the banquet. Got something to talk to you about, eh, Jim? (*He gives* CONOVER *a wink, then to* GRANT) That was a hell of a good speech you made in Wichita. I could go along with two-thirds of it—especially that stuff about strikes. The other third—I suppose you've got to say those things—but look out people don't get the idea you're too far to the left. Talk to you about it later.

MARY

(*Into the telephone*)

Keep trying and call me when you get them. (*She hangs up.*)

SAM

See you later, Mary.

MARY

Good-byc, Sam.

SAM

(*Shaking hands with* GRANT)

Damn it, Grant! I'll be telling people I knew you when.

GRANT

Don't tell them yet!

SAM

(*Outside the door*)

Hey, wait! Going down! (GRANT *closes the door after him.*)

CONOVER

(*Accusingly*)

You're talking about reconversion and full employment to-night.

GRANT

Touching on them, among other things. (*He lights a cigarette.*)

CONOVER

What angle are you taking?

GRANT

We talked about it in Washington. You know how I stand.

CONOVER

In Washington you were pretty specific. You're not being that specific here tonight?

GRANT

You're damn right I am!

CONOVER

What are you going to say?

GRANT

I'm going to tell them they did a great job in war production—and they did! But I'm going to remind them there wasn't any risk in that— The Government paid them for it. They had their engineering brains, and plenty of manpower to do the work.

CONOVER

All right. Why don't you let it go at that?

GRANT

Oh, no! I've got to tell them that now they're up against the test. Now they're on their own. They talk about how they want to save the private-enterprise system. All right, now they've got a chance to do it!

CONOVER

(*Agreeably*)

Yes?

GRANT

They're not going to save it by lowering production so they can raise prices. And they're not going to save it by closing down plants to cut down competition. They're not going to save it if they don't work with unions instead of against them. And those babies who are stirring up war veterans to fight labor—I'm going to take their hide off!

CONOVER

Grant, you can't do that!

GRANT

Jim, you know reconversion goes deeper than re-tooling our plants. We need a moral reconversion. Take full employment—I don't mean the Bill—I mean the principle of it.

What's behind most of the opposition to full employment—behind opposing the whole idea of the Government supplying work. To give private enterprise the chance to supply the employment? Nuts! It's to keep prices up on everything but labor. Let labor starve for a while! Jim, there isn't going to be a free-enterprise system if it means that men are free to starve!

CONOVER

Grant, you can't say those things now, and you can't say them here! This town is one of my best sources for silent money!

GRANT

You'll have to take your chances on the silent money, Jim!

MARY

What is silent money?

CONOVER

(*Ignoring her*)

I warn you, Grant, you can't get out on this limb before the nomination.

MARY

People ought to know where he stands before they nominate him.

CONOVER

(*Angrily*)

The people have damn little to say about the nomination. You two have lived in this country all your lives. Haven't you got that through your heads yet? You're not nominated by the people—you're nominated by the politicians! Why?

Because the voters are too damned lazy to vote in the primaries! Well, politicians are not lazy! Remember what happened to Willkie in Wisconsin!

GRANT

They've got to know what I think, Jim! I told you that from the start. I've got to be on record.

CONOVER

All right—but not here—not tonight! Later. When you're out in Nebraska or Oklahoma.

(SPIKE *enters from the right bedroom.*)

SPIKE

O.K., Grant. This is the last group. And are they fruity?

CONOVER

Stall them, Spike. We're discussing something.

GRANT

No, Jim. I'm seeing them. (GRANT *turns to* SPIKE) Who are they?

SPIKE

I don't know. They call themselves the Americans Incorruptible.

GRANT

I never heard of them.

SPIKE

They're dressed for the McKinley campaign. I didn't take their names. The Head Incorruptible is the fat dame with the big cowcatcher.

GRANT

What's their angle? What are they for?

MARY

With a name like that they're not for anything. They're against something.

SPIKE

Yes. (*He takes* GRANT's *cigarette away from him*) Let's take no chances! But remember—they've got votes!

(GRANT *opens the door to the right bedroom, looks in and then turns back to* SPIKE.)

GRANT

They shouldn't have! (*He exits into the right bedroom.* MARY *crosses to the sofa and picks up a newspaper and starts reading the editorial on* GRANT.)

SPIKE

I think I'd better go and air out Parlor B. (*He starts out. The telephone rings.*)

MARY

That's probably Hilda Parrish for me.

SPIKE

(*Into the telephone*)

Hello . . . This is MacManus. (*He shakes head negatively at* MARY) It's for you, Jim. (SPIKE *exits.* CONOVER *goes to the desk and picks up the receiver.*)

CONOVER

(*Into the telephone, casually as though talking to an old political friend*)

Hello. Oh, hello. How are you? (*Pause*) Who told you I was here—Sam? (*Pause*) Where are you? (*Pause*) All right. I'll come up to your room. (*He hangs up and turns to* MARY) Mary, will you tell Grant— (*The telephone rings again.*)

MARY

(*Drops the paper and starts for the telephone*)

That *must* be Hilda.

CONOVER

Tell Grant I'll be right back. (*He exits into the hall.*)

(*The* WAITER *enters with ice cream and coffee; he pours the coffee.*)

MARY

(*Into the telephone*)

Hello . . . Oh, hello, Hilda. (*Pause*) This is Mary . . . Mary Matthews! (*Pause*) Yes. I'm here with Grant. I'm so sorry you're sick. (*Pause*) Well, if it isn't too much for you we'd love to run out for a few minutes after the banquet. (*Pause*) Good. Oh, Grant's busy in the next room with some women. (*She laughs*) No, he's safe. There's a whole committee of them. (*Pause*) All right . . . see you later. Good-bye, dear. (MARY *hangs up and turns to the* WAITER) Have you the check?

WAITER

Yes, Ma'am. (WAITER *hands* MARY *a pencil and offers the check. She starts writing on the check.*)

MARY

I'll write your tip on the check.

WAITER

Is your husband Grant Matthews?

MARY

Yes.

WAITER

He certainly don't pull any punches, does he?

MARY

(*Smiling*)

You said that just in time. (*She writes the tip on the check and hands it to the* WAITER. *He looks at it and smiles broadly.*)

WAITER

Oh, thank you! (*The* WAITER *hurries out.*)

GRANT

(*Entering from the right bedroom, carrying his hat and coat, which he places on a table near the door*)
Well, we've lost the Americans Incorruptible.

MARY

(*Taking a cup of coffee*)

Who were they? What did they want?

GRANT

(*Sitting down to his ice cream and coffee*)

They don't want America to be too harsh on poor little Germany and Japan. We shouldn't have gotten into it in the first place!

MARY

Oh, that crowd! Against war—but we may have to fight the Russians!

GRANT

Exactly! I wound up making a campaign speech for Stalin. (*He looks around*) Where's Jim?

MARY

He'll be back in a minute. He had a telephone call. Grant, what is silent money?

GRANT

Oh, it's a way they get around the Hatch Act.

MARY

What's the Hatch Act?

GRANT

It's a law they passed a few years ago about campaign funds. Only individuals can give money and nobody more than $5,000, and you have to account for how it's spent. It's a very pretty law—and we feel very moral that it's on the books—but it just doesn't work.

MARY

There must have been some reason for passing it.

GRANT

Yes, there was! It had gotten to be a bad situation. But you know how we do things in this country sometimes. When human nature gets to behaving like human nature, they pass a law repealing human nature. But the Hatch Act is too tough. So men who can afford it, walk in and put silent money down on the barrelhead—cash that can't be traced. It's been done by both parties before the law was passed and since. I've told you before, Mary, there's damn little difference between Democrats and Republicans.

MARY

But if silent money's illegal, I don't think you should take it!

GRANT

Oh, I wouldn't take it. That would be Jim's business.

MARY

But, Grant— (*She puts her coffee cup on the table.*)

GRANT

(*Stopping her*)

Now, Mary, we both drank during Prohibition, didn't we? Put it down to political education, the way the PAC does.

(*Seeing she is still troubled*) I can't be too righteous about taking silent money. I've given it.

MARY

If you take money, you have to pay it back some way.

GRANT

(*Indignant*)

Mary! You know damn well I'm not for sale!

MARY

(*Sharply*)

You've arranged that very neatly in your mind, Grant. All they have to do is buy Conover! I warned you the Presidency was a great temptation!

GRANT

(*After a tight-lipped pause*)

You certainly have a gift for making it tough for me.

MARY

(*Distressed with herself*)

I know. I hear myself saying those things. I suppose it's a gift I picked up in exchange for some illusions.

GRANT

(*With sober reasoning*)

Mary, people change. We've both changed. Life does that to you. We would have been happier if we could have stayed the two kids who went on a honeymoon to Victoria. I'm just as unhappy as you are that we didn't. (*There is a pause.* MARY *moves about the room restlessly, then turns the conversation to a less personal subject.*)

MARY

I'm sorry Jim got a line on what you're going to say here.

GRANT

Yes, damn it! I was all keyed up for tonight's speech.

MARY

(*Disturbed*)

Are you going to change it?

GRANT

Oh, no! Don't worry. I'm going to speak my mind about reconversion.

MARY

Grant, you have to! You told labor they had to take the responsibility that goes with their power! You certainly have to be just as frank with business!

GRANT

I'm going to! Jim's argument was just not to say it here in Detroit.

MARY

In Wichita you said what you really believed. (*She goes to* GRANT) Remember the satisfaction it gave you? I hope you feel that way tonight.

GRANT

I'd like to feel that way all the time. But you know your-self, you get into spots where you just can't afford it. (*He turns away.* MARY *realizes* GRANT *is torn between ambition and integrity. She speaks to him quietly and sincerely.*)

MARY

Grant—you know you don't have to be President.

GRANT

(*The big liar*)

Oh—I don't even expect to be! (*Then with deep sincerity*) But I know this much—I could do a lot of good.

MARY

(*Smoothing his hair*)

Well, Grant, you may have to make up your mind whether you want that inner satisfaction or . . .

(CONOVER *enters from the outer hall.*)

GRANT

(*Rising and putting on his coat*)

Hello, where's Spike? It's getting late. We ought to be going.

CONOVER

He may be getting the car around. Grant, before you go, I'd like to pick up where we left off about your speech to-night.

GRANT

Jim, we haven't got time for it. Let's talk about my speech after I've made it.

(SPIKE *enters from the left bedroom.*)

SPIKE

I hate to pull this on you, Grant, but there's one more delegation.

GRANT

To hell with them! Tell them I've left.

SPIKE

(*Handing a slip of paper to* GRANT)
You can't do that. They might see you on your way out.

GRANT

(*Taking the slip and glancing at it*)
Okay. (*He starts for the left bedroom.*)

MARY

Grant, we're the guests of honor. We can't be late.

GRANT

I'll make this short. Get your things, Mary. (GRANT *exits into the left bedroom.*)

SPIKE

Mary, you've got at least five minutes. I'll go down and check up on the police escort. (SPIKE *exits into the outer hall.*)

MARY

It's a wonderful country! You take the police along with you so they can help you break the speed laws. (*She exits into the right bedroom, leaving the door open.* CONOVER *wanders down to the open door.*)

CONOVER

Take your time, Mary. The way you look tonight I want everybody there before you make your entrance.

MARY

(*Offstage*)

Don't be so flattering, Jim, or I'll think you want something from me!

CONOVER

(*Laughing*)

As a matter of fact, I do. I was just going to ask you a favor.

MARY

(*Entering from the right bedroom wearing her evening wrap*)

Fine! What can I do for you?

CONOVER

You're having Sam Parrish to dinner on the seventeenth. Do you mind inviting me, too?

MARY

Why, no. I'd love to have you.

CONOVER

Can I impose on you by inviting some other guests—say four or five?

MARY

(*Hesitating*)

I hadn't planned that kind of a party on the seventeenth but . . .

CONOVER

If Grant's speaking on the twenty-third on International Policy, it may be important for him to see these people first.

(MARY *hesitates again, then comes to a decision.*)

MARY

All right, Jim. I think we can handle it! Do I know any of these people?

CONOVER

Well, you know Sam— And there's one other I'd like to talk to you about. You remember the reason I wanted you to make this trip in the first place?

MARY

(*Tightening*)

Yes, I remember well enough.

CONOVER

Mary, I've been looking into how that talk got started. Mrs. Thorndyke used to be a frequent guest at your house. Then about a year ago she was crossed off your list, but Grant went on seeing her.

MARY

Yes.

CONOVER

Let's kill off those rumors once and for all. I want Mrs. Thorndyke there on the seventeenth.

MARY

(*In cold anger*)

No, Jim! Not in my house! And of all nights not on the seventeenth! It happens to be our wedding anniversary.

CONOVER

(*With some heat*)

Mary, I'm doing my damnedest to go along with Grant, even though he doesn't always go along with me. I need Mrs. Thorndyke there for more reasons than one. Let me win this one, will you?

MARY

Sorry, Jim, that's more than I can take. (*There is a knock on the door*) Come in! (*The* BELLBOY *enters with a radio.*)

BELLBOY

Here's your radio. I had to steal it from another room.

MARY

That's fine. Can you connect it for us?

CONOVER

Let's talk about this some more after the banquet.

(*The* BELLBOY *puts the radio on the desk and plugs it in.* GRANT *enters from the left bedroom.*)

MARY

Ready!

(GRANT *takes a swig of coffee and* MARY *gets his hat. The* BELLBOY *switches on the radio.*)

BELLBOY

Everybody wanted a radio tonight.

GRANT

(*Pleased*)

So?

BELLBOY

Special broadcast from Hollywood—Bob Hope and Jack Benny.

GRANT

Yes, I've got a break tonight, Jim—I'm following Hope and Benny.

MARY

(*Handing* GRANT *his hat*)

After all that nonsense they'll be glad to hear Grant make some sense.

(*The door opens and* SPIKE *sticks his head in.*)

SPIKE

All set? I've got the elevator waiting for you.

MARY

Grant, fix your tie. Listen in, Jim. You'll find out what Grant's talking about!

GRANT

Good-bye, Jim. (GRANT *and* MARY *exit into the hall.*)

CONOVER

Good luck.

(*We hear some music over the radio; then the* BELLBOY *turns it off.* MARY *rushes back in excitement, looking desperately around the room.*)

MARY

Where's my bag, my bag, my bag?

CONOVER

What's that in your hand? (*She looks down and sees her bag in her hand*)

MARY

That's my bag! (*She wheels and runs out.*)

BELLBOY

(*At the radio*)

Works all right. Do you want it on?

CONOVER

No. I can turn a radio on—and off. (*He tips the* BELLBOY, *who thanks him and exits.* CONOVER *takes a chair from the*

145

table and places it at the right of the desk. Then he crosses to the left bedroom, opens the door, and speaks through it) We may as well sit in here and be comfortable! (CONOVER *turns back into the room.* KAY THORNDYKE *enters. She strolls across the room to the chair by the desk, places her furs and hat on the desk and sits down.* CONOVER *draws up a chair)* I have a radio. Do I dare listen?

KAY

I think so. Of course, I had less than five minutes with him.

CONOVER

Yes. And Mary's had five weeks! (*He lights a cigar.*)

KAY

(*Confidently*)
I think he was glad to see me. I told you in Washington I could handle him.

CONOVER

Well, we'll find out. (*He sits down.*)

KAY

I made it pretty strong. I said the Democrats would never take a chance like that. But that brought up a question that's on his mind, Jim, and you'd better have an answer ready for him.

CONOVER

An answer to what?

KAY

Is there any real difference between the Democratic Party and the Republican Party?

CONOVER

All the difference in the world. (*He turns on the radio*) They're in—and we're out!

Curtain

ACT THREE

ACT THREE

Scene I

*The living room of the Matthews' apartment in New York.
It is a fairly large room, the entrance from the hall being from
an arch upstage, left of center; the door from the elevator is
somewhere offstage left. In this left arch we see stairs leading
to an upper floor. Right of center there is a corresponding
arch. Recessed behind this arch is an alcove bar with bottles
of liquor and glasses, and it is through this arch that the guests
proceed to the dining room, which is off right. Downstage
left there is a single door leading to a powder room and a
place for the ladies' wraps.*

*There is a fireplace in the right wall. There is a small table
and an ottoman below the fireplace. On a line with the fireplace and facing the audience is an upholstered couch. On
stage left there are two comfortable upholstered chairs with a
small table between them. Upstage between the two arches,
there is a cabinet with single chairs at either end. On the
cabinet is a vase of flowers, and above it on the wall hangs a
painting of* MARY *and the two children.*

SPIKE *is sitting on the sofa, his hat beside him. On the floor
at his feet are an ashtray and a package which obviously
contains a bottle of liquor. He has a piece of paper in his
hand and a pencil.*

SWENSON, *the butler, is standing facing* SPIKE, *with a piece
of note-paper in his hand and a pencil.*

SPIKE

(*Consulting the slip of paper he holds*)

Judge Alexander—bourbon—bourbon and plain water—he may take a cocktail, but I doubt it—he'll probably stick to straight bourbon.

SWENSON

Yes, sir. (*He makes a note.*)

SPIKE

Now his wife—do you know how to mix a Sazarac?

SWENSON

No, sir, but I can look it up.

SPIKE

Well, I'll tell you. Take an old-fashioned glass and put a lump of sugar in it, soaked in Pernod.

SWENSON

I don't think we have any Pernod, sir.

SPIKE

I brought some. It's in there. (*He points to the package*) Then a jigger of bourbon, a twist of lemon peel on the top and give it a good stir. Don't sample that one, Swenson, it'll light up your vest buttons. (SWENSON *makes a note*) That's all Mrs. Alexander drinks, but she drinks a lot of them. It's all right for her to get tight, if she wants to—but take it easy on the rest of them. We want to keep them sober. The

Senator likes martinis before dinner, then he goes on a steady diet of Scotch and sodas.

SWENSON

Yes, sir.

SPIKE

Now, Mr. Parrish . . .

SWENSON

Manhattans for Mr. Parrish, and then rye.

SPIKE

And Mrs. Thorndyke—?

SWENSON

Mrs. Thorndyke likes a martini before dinner—very dry.

SPIKE

All right, give her one. Same for Mrs. Draper. Just have plenty of martinis and Manhattans—and Scotch and soda for Mr. Conover. And remember, Swenson, except for Mrs. Alexander nobody gets too much to drink—and that goes for Mr. and Mrs. Matthews too.

(GRANT *has entered through the left arch during the last sentence of* SPIKE's *speech. He is wearing a hat and a topcoat, and carries a small wrapped box. He drops the hat and the box on a chair.*)

153

GRANT

What goes for Mr. and Mrs. Matthews?

SPIKE

I'm straightening Swenson out on the drinks—and nobody's
to get too many. If there's one thing I don't want around here
tonight, it's too much frankness—especially from you. I'm
thinking of that time you got tight in San Francisco. We'd
been in a hell of a fix if the newspaper men hadn't gotten
drunker. Swenson wanted to know where to put the place
cards. I've got a diagram here. (SPIKE *takes a piece of card-
board out of his pocket.*)

GRANT

Wait till I get Mary. (*He hurries up the stairs.*)

SWENSON

There's a Mr. Hardy on the list, sir.

SPIKE

Those labor boys are smart cookies. He doesn't drink anything.

(SWENSON *picks up the package at* SPIKE's *feet and goes
through the right arch to the bar. He leaves the package behind the bar and exits right. We hear* GRANT *before we see him.*)

GRANT

Well, make it as soon as you can. I'm late. I should be
changing. (*He comes downstairs, taking off his topcoat and*

holding it over his arm) She'll be here in a minute. (GRANT *goes to the fireplace.*)

SPIKE

Nervous about tonight?

GRANT

Yes, a little. I feel as though I'm being quietly surrounded.

SPIKE

Take it easy. Let them do the talking.

GRANT

Oh, I'm not making any commitments here tonight. You and Jim and I are meeting over at Kay's after they've gone.

SPIKE

Look, they're going to throw the book at you tonight. That goes for Conover too. They don't expect you to take it all— it's just as Kay said last night—they'll be willing to compromise.

GRANT

Before I got into this, it all seemed so clear and simple. I suppose it does to almost everybody who doesn't have to make the decisions.

SPIKE

Yeah, Mary, for instance.

GRANT

I know now it isn't just black and white—but damn it, where do you draw the line? (*He thinks a moment*) I know damn well once I got to be President— (*A pause*) Well!

SPIKE

I'll drop back about midnight and pick you up and we can talk it out at Kay's.

GRANT

Spike, keep that to yourself—we're supposed to be meeting . . .

(MARY *enters down the stairs. She is in evening dress. There is a lack of warmth between her and* GRANT.)

MARY
(*Crossing to arm of sofa and sitting*)
Hello, Spike. I'm sorry to get you up here, but I told Grant you had to help seat these people.

SPIKE

I've got a diagram here. (*He shows* MARY *the diagram*) You're here—and Grant's at the other end.

GRANT
(*Sitting on the sofa beside* SPIKE)
Well, if we're going to observe any protocol, Senator Lauterback ranks. I think he ought to be on Mary's right.

SPIKE

Okay, and I'll put Mrs. Draper on your right. We're short of women, some of the men will have to sit together.

MARY

Why don't you put Sam Parrish on Grant's left?

GRANT

Don't you want Sam up near you? It'll give you someone to talk to.

MARY

Well, I thought that after what you *didn't* say about reconversion in Detroit, you and Sam might want to hold hands under the table.

GRANT

Mary, we've been over that often enough. I *did* talk about reconversion in Detroit.

MARY

I wouldn't say about it, Grant. I'd say around it. You did come right out and mention the word once.

GRANT

(*Rising, and speaking with angry finality*)
Mary, I've heard all I want to hear about Detroit.

SPIKE

(*To the rescue*)
Here's a good couple to pair off. Hardy and Mrs. Alexander. He never opens his mouth and she never closes hers. (*He writes their names down*) How about Mrs. Thorndyke up here? (*He points to one end of the diagram.*)

MARY

How about Mrs. Thorndyke down there? (*She points to the other end of the diagram.*)

157

SPIKE

Okay. Then the Judge here, and Jim here. (*He writes and then holds up the diagram*) That looks all right. (*He hands it to* MARY.)

GRANT

(*Looking at his watch*)

Hell, I've got to get dressed. (*He starts for the stairs.*)

MARY

Grant, you're looking in on Sonny and Joyce?

GRANT

I certainly am. (*He goes back to* MARY) Mary, I know this dinner isn't going to be much fun for you. It's damn nice of you to do it for me. I appreciate it.

MARY

Nonsense, Grant. I hope it's everything you want it to be. I'll do my best. Just to show you how serious I am about it, I'm not even going to have a cocktail.

GRANT

I'm going light myself. (*He starts off, then notices his hat and the box on the chair. He picks them up*) Oh, Mary, I almost forgot. This is for tonight. (*He hands her the box and hurries upstairs.* MARY *rises and watches* GRANT *as he leaves.*)

MARY

I didn't think he even remembered it.

SPIKE

Remembered what?

MARY

Today's our wedding anniversary. Excuse me, Spike! (*She takes off the wrapping eagerly, revealing a box of cigars*) My error! (JENNY, *a maid, enters from the right arch*) Jenny!

JENNY

Yes, Madam?

MARY

Here's the table diagram. Will you take care of the place cards? And these cigars?

JENNY

(*Taking both diagram and cigars*)

Very good, Madam. (JENNY *exits left into the hall.*)

SPIKE

(*With forced gaiety*)

Those cigars are Llaranaguas, the only brand Conover smokes. Don't tell me Grant doesn't know how to play politics.

MARY

Oh, I know he plays politics! I've found that out! (*In unhappy puzzlement*) I *wish* I knew *why* he changed his speech in Detroit!

SPIKE

(*Casually*)

Jim talked to him, didn't he? Warned him not to say anything that would cost us any campaign contributions?

MARY

No, Spike, it wasn't for money. So if you do know, you won't tell me. You're not on my team. And I've often wondered why. You know, Spike, you've got a very wide streak of decency.

SPIKE

Yes, and if I don't watch it, it gets in my way. (*Seriously*) Mary, I'll pull every trick I know to get Grant in the White House, but once he's there and I'm back on the newspaper, I'll be on the same team with you; and if Grant isn't in there pitching for the people, I'll burn his pants off!

MARY

I'll light the matches for you.

SPIKE

(*Rising*)

But don't start any bonfires here tonight. (JENNY *crosses the hall, on her way to the outer door*) These educated apes that are coming here—Grant can't be nominated without their support, and in the election they can deliver a lot of votes.

MARY

(*Scornfully*)

How can you deliver the votes of a free people?

SPIKE

Mary, lazy people and ignorant people and prejudiced people are not free.

(*We hear the voice of* JUDGE ALEXANDER *offstage.*)

ALEXANDER
(*Offstage*)

Is Mrs. Matthews in?

JENNY
(*Offstage*)

This way, sir.

SPIKE

(*Picking up the ashtray and putting it on the table*)
Somebody's here. I'd better run. I'll be back in time to help
you sweep them out.

MARY

Wait until whoever this is comes in, will you, Spike? I
don't know them all.

(JUDGE JEFFERSON DAVIS ALEXANDER *and* MRS. LULUBELLE
ALEXANDER *enter. She is still wearing her wrap, which she
hands to* JENNY *who exits with it to room down left.
The* ALEXANDERS *are from the deep South. He is tall
and lean. She is short and plump.*)

SPIKE

(*Holding out his hand*)
Hello, Judge. I'm Spike MacManus. Remember me?

ALEXANDER

(*Expansively, crossing to shake hands with* SPIKE)
Indeed I do! It's a great pleasure to see you again, sir!
This is Mrs. Alexander.

SPIKE

How do you do? Mrs. Matthews, this is Judge Alexander and Mrs. Alexander.

MARY

(*Holding out her hand*)

How do you do, Judge Alexander?

ALEXANDER

(*Shaking hands*)

It's an honor to be here, Mrs. Matthews.

MARY

(*To* LULUBELLE)

I'm especially glad you could come, Mrs. Alexander. We women are going to be outnumbered here tonight.

LULUBELLE

That's nothing new to me, Mrs. Matthews. When I go to dinner with the Judge's Republican friends I'm always out-numbered. I make it a point to tell my hostess right off that while Jeff's a Republican, I'm a Democrat. But you can speak freely. You Republicans can't say anything about the Admin-istration mean enough for us Democrats down South. (LULU-BELLE *laughs; she is incurably good-natured.*)

SPIKE

(*Amused*)

I'll leave you my proxy, Mrs. Alexander. I've got to run along. Good night. Good night, Mary. Good night, Judge. (SPIKE *exits left.*)

ALEXANDER

(*Calling after him heartily*)

It's been very pleasant seeing you again, sir! Good night!
(*He turns to* MARY) Who is he?

MARY

A newspaperman. He's been helping my husband. Won't
you sit down?

(LULUBELLE *goes to one of the easy chairs and sits.*
JENNY *enters from the room down left and exits through
the arch toward the outer door.*)

MARY

Mr. Matthews will be down in a minute.

ALEXANDER

Mrs. Alexander and I are certainly looking forward to meeting him.

(SWENSON *enters from the left arch and stands await-
ing* MARY'S *orders.*)

MARY

You must be looking forward to a cocktail, too.

LULUBELLE

Frankly, I'm looking forward to both.

SWENSON

(*To* ALEXANDER)

Bourbon, sir?

ALEXANDER

You read my mind.

LULUBELLE

He can't read my mind.

SWENSON

(*Turning to* LULUBELLE)

A Sazarac, I believe?

ALEXANDER

Lulubelle, your reputation's getting too far north.

MARY

Swenson, can you make a Sazarac?

SWENSON

I think so, Ma'am.

LULUBELLE

If he just thinks so, Jeff, you'd better mix that Sazarac.

ALEXANDER

Yes, honey.

MARY

(*Indicating*)

The bar's right over there.

SWENSON

This way, sir. (*He leads* ALEXANDER *to the alcove bar, where the* JUDGE *goes to work mixing a Sazarac.*)

MARY

Do you get up North often?

LULUBELLE

Being a Republican down South, the Judge only gets important every four years, around Convention time. Jim Conover getting him way up here this early must mean they're pretty serious about running your husband for President, which I hope they don't.

MARY

Really?

LULUBELLE

Yes, you seem like such a nice woman. Politics is too good an excuse for a man to neglect his wife.

MARY

Well, if you're neglected tonight—you and I will be neglected together. (*She hears voices in the hall and moves up to greet the new guests.*)

(JENNY *ushers in* MRS. GRACE DRAPER *and* JIM CONOVER. *They are followed by* BILL HARDY, *and later* SENATOR LAUTERBACK. MRS. DRAPER *is a positive woman whose mind has been closed ever since Roosevelt's first term.* CONOVER *is dressed in a conservative business suit.* BILL HARDY, *the labor leader, obviously hasn't just come from the factory. He is dressed in dinner clothes and wishes he weren't.* SENATOR LAUTERBACK *represents the farm bloc, but has been doing his farming in the Senate for a great many years.* JENNY *takes* MRS. DRAPER'S *wrap and exits with it into the room downstage left.*)

CONOVER

Hello, Mary. This is Mrs. Draper, Mrs. Matthews. Hello, Lulubelle. Where's the Judge?

LULUBELLE

Mixing me a drink.

CONOVER

Well, this is where I went out. (*He waves to the* JUDGE) Hello, Judge!

ALEXANDER

(*From the bar*)

Hello, Jim!

MRS. DRAPER

(*Crossing to* MARY *and shaking hands*)

I've been so eager to meet you and your husband.

MARY

It's so nice that you could come. Do you know Mrs. Alexander?

(MRS. DRAPER *goes to* LU-LUBELLE.)

CONOVER

Mrs. Matthews, this is Bill Hardy.

(HARDY *shakes hands with* MARY.)

MARY

Hello, Mr. Hardy.

HARDY

(*Aggrieved*)

Nobody told me not to dress.

MRS. DRAPER

(*To* LULUBELLE)

You're Judge Alexander's wife. I met you in Chicago.

LULUBELLE

Oh, yes, at the Convention. I was so glad to get back down South away from that heat.

(MRS. DRAPER *crosses to the sofa and sits down.* SWENSON *has entered from the bar with a tray of drinks.*)

CONOVER

My fault, Bill. I slipped up on that.

MARY

I'm glad you did dress. Men are getting all too lazy about dressing.

CONOVER

Isn't that what you're after, Bill? Put labor in evening clothes and let the rest of us go without? Have a drink! (*He points to the bar*) Oh, Mary, this is Senator Lauterback.

SENATOR

(*Shaking hands with* MARY)

Wanted to meet you ever since you made that trip with your husband. You were just as big a hit as he was. He talks well, but you're prettier.

CONOVER

Mr. Matthews will be down
in a minute, Senator, and the
bar's over there.

(*The* SENATOR *goes to the bar.*)

MARY

(*As* SWENSON *comes up with the tray*)
You want a highball, don't you, Jim?

CONOVER

Well, we've just come from a little caucus in my room
at the hotel. We did some drinking there. Oh, all right. (*He
takes a highball.* SWENSON *turns to offer a drink to* MARY.)

MARY

No, thank you, Swenson. I'm not having anything to drink
tonight. (SWENSON *serves a drink to* MRS. DRAPER. KAY THORN-
DYKE *enters and stands in the left arch.* MARY *turns and sees
her. There is a moment of tension*) Hello, Kay.

KAY

Hello, Mary. (KAY *walks forward with outstretched hand*)
You're looking very pretty tonight.

MARY

(*Taking a martini from* SWENSON'S *tray and putting it
in* KAY'S *outstretched hand.*)
You're just in time for a cocktail. Do you know everyone
here?

KAY

I know Mrs. Draper.

(*The* JUDGE *has entered from the bar with* LULUBELLE's *Sazarac, which he takes to her. The* SENATOR *and* BILL HARDY *remain at the bar.*)

MARY

Mrs. Alexander, this is Mrs. Thorndyke—and Judge Alexander.

KAY

How do you do?

LULUBELLE

Hello, Mrs. Thorndyke. (LULUBELLE *starts her drinking.*)

ALEXANDER

Mrs. Thorndyke, I'm very pleased to meet you. I was raised in the old traditions of the South, where it was looked down on for a woman to go into anything like newspaper business. But no gentleman of the South could deny as attractive a woman as you your outstanding success. Which reminds me of a story! A number of years ago when I was a small boy . . .

LULUBELLE

Jeff, this is the best Sazarac I ever had in my life. Mix me another one right away!

ALEXANDER

Yes, honey.

169

MRS. DRAPER

Kay, after you left, Jim and I went into the situation in Chicago. Jim, tell her what you said.

KAY

Oh, Grace, let's take time out of politics for a little drinking. You're in for a bad evening, Mary.

(*The* JUDGE, *having lost his audience, goes to the bar.*)

MARY

Oh, no! Politics is new to me, but I'm very interested.

CONOVER
(*Amiably, but sardonically*)

You've got the "very" in the wrong place, Mary. Interested, but very new.

MARY
(*To the others, smiling*)

Mr. Conover means I haven't lost my amateur standing.

CONOVER

You're learning—I hope!

MARY

That's a dangerous hope, Jim. You politicians have stayed professionals because the voters have remained amateurs.

(SAM PARRISH *appears in the left arch.*)

SAM

Hello, everybody! Late as usual! Had a hell of a day! (*He goes to* MARY) How's my sweetheart?

MARY

Hello, Sam.

(SAM *kisses her.*)

SAM

That's for Hilda! (*He kisses her again*) That's for me! (*Hearing* SAM, HARDY *and the* SENATOR *drift into the room*) Jim, I won't get down to Washington until afternoon. How about dinner instead of lunch?

CONOVER

That suits me even better.

SENATOR

Hello, Sam.

SAM

Senator! You'll be glad to hear I'm starting a back-to-the-farm movement. Just closed down two plants. (HARDY *steps into view from behind the* SENATOR) Oh, hello, Bill! Shouldn't have said that in front of you! Mary, do I have to sit down with Labor again tonight? Where's Grant?

MARY

He'll be down any minute.

MRS. DRAPER

Hello, Sam!

SAM

Hello, Grace!

MARY

Do you know Mrs. Alexander? Mr. Parrish.

SAM

How are you, Mrs. Alexander?

MARY

And have you met Mrs. Thorndyke?

KAY

Oh, yes, we know each other. Nice seeing you, Mr. Parrish.

SAM

(*To* KAY)

Where did you get to that night? I looked all over the banquet hall for you.

KAY

(*After a second's pause*)

I didn't go to the banquet.

CONOVER

(*To change the subject*)

Say, how's Hilda?

SAM

She's fine now. Mrs. Thorndyke, I thought that was why you were in Detroit—to hear Grant's speech.

MARY

Were you in Detroit when we were there, Kay?

SAM

Yes, you must have seen her, Mary. She was on her way to your suite. I'd just left you, remember?

MARY

I didn't see Mrs. Thorndyke in Detroit. (*Fitting the pieces together*) Oh, you must have dropped in to talk to Grant about reconversion.

SAM

What Grant said about reconversion in his speech that night was all right. You couldn't argue with it.

MARY

Well, I think you can thank Mrs. Thorndyke for that.

CONOVER

(*Interrupting and going center to* SAM)
Sam, did you get that finance report I sent you?

SAM	KAY
Yes, and it's a damn bad job. I've made you a whole new list. (*He searches through his pockets.*)	(*To* MRS. DRAPER) Grace, I'm having another cocktail.

MRS. DRAPER

I'll have one, too.

(*They both go to the bar.*)

173

MARY
(*Turning to* CONOVER)
Well, Jim, you hoped I'd learn. I'm learning.

(*The* JUDGE *enters from the bar with two Sazaracs and goes to* LULUBELLE.)

SAM
Left it in my overcoat. I'll get it. (*He starts out and sees the* JUDGE) Hello, Judge! You drinking with both hands now?

ALEXANDER
Hello, Sam! These aren't for me. (SAM *exits into the hall. The* JUDGE *places the drinks on the table beside* LULUBELLE) Honey, I want to talk to some of these people, so I brought you two of them.

LULUBELLE
Thank you, Jeff. (*She takes a fresh drink.*)

MARY
Judge, I'll have one of those.

(*The* JUDGE *hands her a drink.*)

CONOVER
(*Concerned*)
Mary, those are pretty powerful. I thought you weren't drinking anything tonight.

MARY
(Incisively)
I've just been reconverted! (*She takes a healthy swallow.*)

LULUBELLE
Jeff, make another one for me right away.

ALEXANDER
Yes, honey. (*He starts for the bar.*)

MARY
Hm-m, I like these. Judge, would you make another one
for me too? (MARY *sits in the comfortable chair next to* LULU-
BELLE. *The* JUDGE *starts toward the bar.* GRANT MATTHEWS *comes
down the stairs into the arch as* SAM *enters from the left with
a sheaf of papers in his hand.*)

GRANT
Hello, Sam!
SAM
Grant! All I've got to decide tonight is whether we're go-
ing to run you for a third term.

(*They shake hands and come into the room together.*)

CONOVER
How're you, Grant? You certainly took time to pretty
yourself up.
GRANT
Was it successful? Sorry I'm late.

(*The* JUDGE *has crossed down in front of sofa.*)

ALEXANDER

Mr. Matthews, I'm Judge Alexander.

GRANT

(*With a gesture*)

Not guilty! (*He crosses to the* JUDGE *and they shake hands.* SAM *takes* CONOVER *aside into conference.*)

ALEXANDER

Sir, I reject your plea. I'm sentencing you to four years in the White House!

GRANT

(*Laughing*)

You're taking Jim Conover more seriously than I am.

(MARY *and* LULUBELLE *are drinking steadily.*)

ALEXANDER

Mr. Conover's a man to be taken seriously. Due to his efforts I almost had the honor of being the last man appointed to public office by Herbert Hoover. But the Federal Judge we expected to die held on a few days and the first thing we knew Mr. Roosevelt was in office. So I'm still on the State bench. However, my term expires in 1948. So . . .

LULUBELLE

Jeff!

ALEXANDER

Yes, honey?

LULUBELLE

I'm going to be needing my other drink.

ALEXANDER

Yes, honey.

MARY

Grant, this is Mrs. Alexander.

(GRANT *turns to* LULUBELLE. *Again without an audience, the* JUDGE *returns to the bar.*)

GRANT

How do you do, Mrs. Alexander?

LULUBELLE

(*To* MARY)

Handsome, isn't he? *He's* the first good reason I've ever seen for voting Republican. (*To* GRANT) I warned your wife I was a Democrat.

GRANT

Some of my best friends are Democrats.

LULUBELLE

Well, you know us Southerners. We vote Democratic at home, but we've got an awfully good Republican record in Congress.

(KAY, MRS. DRAPER, HARDY *and the* SENATOR *come in from the bar.* SWENSON *arrives at this moment at* GRANT's *side with a tray of drinks.* GRANT *takes a martini and turns to* MARY.)

GRANT

Cocktail, Mary? Oh, you're not drinking anything, are you?

177

MARY

(*Holding glass aloft*)

Yes! Sazaracs!

GRANT

(*Surprised*)

Oh?

KAY

Hello, Grant!

(GRANT *turns and goes to her.*)

GRANT

Oh, hello, Kay! Nice seeing you again.

(*They shake hands.*)

KAY

Do you know Bill Hardy?

GRANT

Glad you're here, Mr. Hardy.

HARDY

Nobody told me not to dress. (*He shakes hands with* GRANT, *then turns to the fireplace to nurse his sense of social injustice.*)

KAY

And this is Grace Draper.

GRANT

I've been looking forward to meeting you, Mrs. Draper. You're on the National Committee, I believe.

KAY

And they're going to run Mrs. Draper for Congress.

GRANT

Fine! I always say a woman's place is in the House.

SENATOR

(*Coming down to* GRANT)

Just so they stay out of the Senate. How are you, Mr. Matthews? I'm Senator Lauterback.

(*They shake hands.*)

GRANT

Oh, of course.

(CONOVER *comes down and joins the group.*)

SENATOR

We met before, in a manner of speaking. Remember? You testified before my Committee. You made a very strong impression on us.

GRANT

(*Amused*)

Well, I would never have guessed it from the Committee's report.

CONOVER

The Senator was just telling me about that, Grant. He can give you the inside on it. I think you'll find it very interesting.

(SWENSON *approaches the group around* GRANT *with a tray of drinks.*)

GRANT

Senator, we'll have to go into that later. I'd like to hear about it. Another cocktail, Mrs. Draper?

MRS. DRAPER

Thank you. They're very good. (*She takes one.*)

GRANT

How about you, Kay?

KAY

No, two's my limit.

GRANT

How about you, Senator? Or would you rather have a highball?

LULUBELLE

(*To* MARY)

You see, that's what happens when your husband gets into politics. You just sit off in a corner.

MARY

We have each other for company tonight and it gives us time to attend to our drinking. (*She finishes her Sazarac just as the* JUDGE *arrives with two more. Both women take fresh drinks.*)

LULUBELLE

Just in time, Jeff. Fix us some more right away.

ALEXANDER

SENATOR

No, I'll stick to these. (*He takes a cocktail*) And very good too!

Honey, there are a lot of things I want to talk to Mr. Matthews about.

LULUBELLE

GRANT

(*To* HARDY)

Want that refreshed, Mr. Hardy?

Mix the drinks before you start talkin', Jeff; you know how I hate to interrupt you.

ALEXANDER

Yes, honey.

HARDY

No, you can drink just so much Coca-Cola.

(JUDGE *hurries back to bar, muttering.*)

(SWENSON *returns to bar and then disappears into dining room.*)

KAY

Grant, Mrs. Draper is very interested in what you plan to say at the Foreign Policy Association Thursday night.

GRANT

(*To* MRS. DRAPER)

Yes, Thursday's the night I settle world affairs.

KAY

Grace is the Party's expert on the foreign vote.

181

MRS. DRAPER

I think the election in '46 is going to turn on it, and in '48 too.

KAY

Take the Italians, for instance. Everybody knows we've made a mess of things in Italy.

MRS. DRAPER

The Italians over here are all unhappy about it, and they're going to be even unhappier when the final peace terms are drawn up.

KAY

Truman has to take responsibility for the peace terms. So it's not going to be hard to appeal to the Italian vote.

GRANT

I think we have to wait and find out what the peace terms are.

KAY

We don't have to wait. We just have to demand justice for Italy.

MARY

(*Who has been listening to this, speaks up, with Sazarac-inspired articulateness*)
If you favor Italy, won't that lose you the Abyssinian vote?

MRS. DRAPER

(*Turning to* MARY)
Mrs. Matthews, there isn't any Abyssinian vote.

MARY

Good! We don't have to worry about justice for the Abyssinians. (MARY *goes back to her drinking.*)

KAY

(*To* GRANT)

Grace thinks that in this election the Polish vote is the most important.

MRS. DRAPER

Indeed I do! Now in your speech Thursday night you should come out for the reopening of the whole Polish question—boundaries, government, reparations—

KAY

Any strong stand, Grant, would clinch the Polish vote.

MARY

I thought the Poles voted in Poland.

KAY

(*To* MARY, *kindly*)

We're talking about Polish-Americans.

MARY

Oh, can you be both?

SAM

(*Looking up from his papers*)

Mary, you're a sweet girl and I love you, but this is practical politics, and you're way out over your head.

MARY

If they're Americans I should think you'd ask them to vote as Americans, not as Poles!

GRANT

(*Too heartily*)

Mary, I think we could all use some more hors d'oeuvres.

(MARY *rises and goes to bell in the left wall, which she presses.*)

KAY

Take Pennsylvania for instance . . .

MARY

Is this what's called power politics?

SENATOR

(*Strolling toward* MARY)

Mrs. Matthews, power politics is what they play in Europe.

MARY

(*Crossing back to her chair*)

It seems to me we're beginning to play it right here. Let's disunite the United Nations and keep Pennsylvania safe for the Republicans. (*She sits.* JUDGE ALEXANDER *comes out of the bar with a tray holding four Sazaracs. He crosses to* LULU-BELLE.)

ALEXANDER

Doggone it, I miss everything. Who says we're not going to carry Pennsylvania? (*He places the tray on the table and addresses* LULUBELLE) Honey, I made four this time. I'm missing out on everything. I'm starved for some good Republican talk.

(JENNY *enters from left arch in answer to bell.* MARY *and* LULUBELLE *each take a fresh Sazarac.*)

LULUBELLE
(*Raising her glass to* MARY)
More power to you!

MARY
Thanks! They're full of it, aren't they? (MARY *starts on her third Sazarac.*)

GRANT
(*To* JENNY)
Jenny, some hors d'oeuvres please.

(JENNY *takes a tray of hors d'oeuvres from a table at the foot of the stairs and passes them.*)

ALEXANDER
Mr. Matthews, if I may say so, I think you're the hope of the new South.

SENATOR
Here we go again! The Judge is going to promise that we'll break the solid South.

ALEXANDER
Senator, you don't understand the conditions down there!

SENATOR

All I have to say is that when a State votes the same way for one hundred years, it's a reflection on the intelligence of the electorate. (*Turns to* MARY) Don't you agree with me, Mrs. Matthews?

MARY

I'm from Vermont. (*She drinks.*)

SENATOR

That's not the same thing. Vermont's always been a good sound Republican State. (*To* GRANT) Mr. Matthews, in your speech Thursday I know you have to tie up world peace with tariff reductions and we realize industry has to make some sacrifices along that line . . .

SAM

Oh, industry has to make the sacrifices!

SENATOR

But I think you'll have to reassure the American farmer that he won't be forced to compete with Russian wheat and Danish butter and Argentine beef.

GRANT

Senator, there's a direct connection between world trade and world peace.

KAY

Grant, the farmer has a special case.

SENATOR

And twenty million votes!

GRANT

Senator, I want you to talk to me very, very frankly and very fully, and give me all the information you can—but please don't expect me to make any decisions here tonight.

MARY

That's the way Grant works. He likes to listen to people before he makes any decish—(MARY *stops short, looks down at the drink, puts the drink on the table, then continues somewhat defiantly*)—before he decides anything.

SAM

I thought we were going to talk turkey tonight. If I'm going to raise this money, I've got to take word back to Detroit how Grant stands on certain issues.

CONOVER

(*Following* SAM *down to center*)

After you've gone, Grant and I are going to hold a caucus. We'll have word for all of you tomorrow.

SENATOR

(*To* SAM)

Sam, Mr. Matthews' strength is with big business. Why should they be worried about him?

SAM

You know what we're worried about. Are we going to be in for a lot of government competition, or is this country going to be put back in the hands of private enterprise?

(SWENSON *enters from arch left and tries to catch* MARY's *eye.*)

MARY

(*Rising*)

Oh, Grant believes in private enterprise. (*She stares across at* KAY) Doesn't he, Kay?

SWENSON

Dinner is served, Ma'am.

(SWENSON *exits.*)

GRANT

Dinner. Good! Take your cocktails with you if you haven't finished. (*He crosses to center*) Mary!

MARY

(*Leading the guests out*)

Just find your own place cards. I hope some of you men don't mind sitting together. There aren't enough women to go around. (MARY *exits through the right arch, followed by* MRS. DRAPER *and* LULUBELLE, *then* HARDY, ALEXANDER, SAM, SENATOR *and* CONOVER. KAY *delays following the others so that when all are gone but* GRANT *she can seize the opportunity to speak to him.*)

KAY

(With cold anger)

Grant, Mary's tight. Is there any way you can talk to her—do something with her?

GRANT

(Worried)

What happened?

KAY

It was Sam. The minute he walked into the room he . . .

(MARY *enters from dining room, speaking back over her shoulder.*)

MARY

Find your place cards, everyone. I forgot my—(*She turns and sees* GRANT *and* KAY)—cocktail.

(KAY *brushes past her to dining room.* MARY *stares after her.*)

GRANT

Mary, I'm depending on you to help me tonight.

MARY

(Crossing to the table)

I'm afraid I interrupted you and Kay before she had a chance to tell you what you think. (*She picks up drink from table.*)

GRANT

Leave that drink here, and get some food into you as soon as you can!

MARY

(*Challengingly*)

Well! Seems to me you're getting a little belligerel.

GRANT

Mary, I'm on a spot here tonight. We both are. We have to be ready to do some quick thinking.

MARY

(*Starting for the dining room*)

Don't worry about me. (*She stops and looks back at* GRANT) I'm a very thick quinker. (MARY *continues toward the dining room, walking with careful deliberation.* GRANT *starts to follow.*)

Curtain

ACT III

Scene II

The same, some time after dinner.
MARY and LULUBELLE are seated in the comfortable chairs.
MARY is drinking coffee with a certain desperation.
On the table between them is LULUBELLE's demitasse, un-
touched. LULUBELLE is at work on a bourbon and soda. MARY
finishes her coffee, puts it down on the table and notices LULU-
BELLE's full cup. She eyes it for a second and then speaks to
LULUBELLE.

MARY

You haven't touched your coffee.

LULUBELLE

Never use it. Keeps me awake nights.

MARY
(Picking up the cup)

Do you mind?

LULUBELLE

Help yourself, honey.

(MARY starts on LULUBELLE's coffee. LULUBELLE is sipping
her highball as though her immediate memories gave
her some amusement. SWENSON appears with a coffee

pot on a tray. He approaches the empty cup which MARY
has put down.)

SWENSON

(*To* LULUBELLE)

More coffee, Ma'am?

MARY

(*Promptly*)

Yes, Swenson.

(*He fills the empty cup, then turns to* MARY.)

SWENSON

Coffee, Ma'am?

MARY

Yes, please. (*She quickly finishes coffee in her cup, then
holds it out for* SWENSON *to refill*) Be sure everyone in the
dining room is taken care of. And did you remember Mr.
Conover's cigars?

SWENSON

Yes, Ma'am. (SWENSON *starts back to the dining room.* MRS.
DRAPER *enters. He allows her to pass and then exits.* MRS.
DRAPER *heads for the powder room, but stops center and points
toward it.*)

MRS. DRAPER

Am I right?

(MARY *nods, giving her the best smile she can muster.*
MRS. DRAPER *hurries into the powder room.*)

LULUBELLE

(*To* MARY, *reassuringly*)

I thought she spoke to you real friendly.

MARY

Shouldn't she have? What did I say to *her?*

LULUBELLE

I can't quite remember, honey, but it was followed by one of the loudest silences I've ever heard.

(MARY *suffers and gulps some coffee.*)

MARY

I can't remember anything that happened before the salad.

LULUBELLE

You missed the best part. You certainly were whamming away at them. You picked them off one by one—like settin' birds. I haven't enjoyed myself so much since Huey Long died.

MARY

(*After taking another gulp of coffee*)

Can you remember any of the things I said?

LULUBELLE

(*Thinking*)

Now let me see—what was it you said to the Senator? I kept wishing I had a pencil so I could write 'em down. It may come back to me later. That was the time Sam Parrish had the choking spell. You remember that, don't you?

MARY

(*Disconsolately*)

No.

LULUBELLE

Oh, he had to leave the table. Then when he came back you started on *him*.

MARY

Oh, dear! (*She puts her empty cup down and takes up* LULUBELLE's *full one and starts drinking from it.*)

LULUBELLE

It was something personal that I couldn't rightly follow. Your husband got it. That's when he knocked over his wine. My!—And that looked like an expensive dress Mrs. Thorndyke is wearing. (MARY *comes out of coffee cup with a broad smile and turns to* LULUBELLE) I don't think she likes you, honey. She was the only one that tried to get back at you. But you took care of her!

MARY

What were they talking about?

LULUBELLE

It was kinda hard to keep track of it, because every time you said something they changed the subject. (MARY *suffers*) After we've gone, you'd better make up to your husband. I don't think he thought that talk about the thermometer was very funny.

MARY
(*Bewildered*)
Thermometer? What thermometer?

LULUBELLE
Oh, you just kept bedeviling him to take his temperature.

MARY
Why?

LULUBELLE
Well, you said he was getting another one of his attacks of gallopin' self-importance. (MARY *winces*) I remember that one! I'm saving that up to use on Jeff! (LULUBELLE *finishes her drink.*)

MARY
I certainly picked a good day for this. (*Turns to* LULUBELLE) It's our wedding anniversary.

LULUBELLE
(*Thoughtfully*)
Well, honey, this is one anniversary you'll both always remember. (JENNY *crosses back of arch toward the outer door.* SWENSON *enters from the dining room with a tray holding a silver coffee pot and a bourbon and soda.* LULUBELLE *helps herself to the highball*) Thank you!

SWENSON
(*Pouring coffee for* MARY)
Shall I leave this here?

MARY

Yes, please. Thanks, Swenson. (*He puts the tray with the coffee-pot on the table.* SPIKE *enters through the arch.*)

SPIKE

(*Blithely*)

Hello, there! How's everything going?

MARY

Just daisy.

(SWENSON *picks up* LULUBELLE's *empty glass and starts to exit.*)

SPIKE

(*To* SWENSON)

Will you tell Mr. Matthews I'm here?

(SWENSON *bows and exits.*)

MARY

They're still in the dining room, talking politics.

SPIKE

Did it get too much for you?

MARY

I got too much for them.

SPIKE

(*Concerned*)

Oh-oh!

MARY

And don't ask for a copy of my speech. No matter what they tell you, I've been misquoted.

(GRANT *appears in the right arch.*)

GRANT

Hello, Spike, come on in! You know everybody.

SPIKE

How's it going?

GRANT

I don't know.

SPIKE

If it's a smoke-filled room, I can tell you—you're nominated. (SPIKE *exits into dining room.* GRANT *looks at his watch. He speaks in* MARY'S *general direction.*)

GRANT

I didn't know it was that late. Spike came to get Jim and me. We're going over to Jim's hotel afterwards for a post-mortem. Swenson taking care of you, Mrs. Alexander?

LULUBELLE

Yes, thank you. We're having a good time in here.

GRANT

We're having a good time in there—now. (GRANT *exits into the dining room.* MARY *hastily drinks more coffee.*)

197

LULUBELLE

You blame it all on me, honey. You tell him I started you drinking those Sazaracs.

MARY

(*Painfully*)

What's in those buzz bombs?

(MRS. DRAPER *enters from the powder room.*)

LULUBELLE

Mrs. Draper, you've given me an idea. (*She rises and exits into the powder room.*)

MARY

(*To* MRS. DRAPER)

Won't you sit down and have a drink with us?

MRS. DRAPER

I have to catch a train. I'm just going back to say my good nights.

(CONOVER *enters from the dining room.*)

CONOVER

Oh, Grace, I was afraid you'd gone. The talk has swung around to your territory. They need some information.

MRS. DRAPER

I can only stay a couple of minutes. (*She exits.* CONOVER *looks at* MARY *thoughtfully.*)

CONOVER

Can I get you a drink?

MARY

Not until about 1952.

CONOVER

Oh, I forgot to tell you. There's been a shake-up in my secret service. I'll prove it to you. The Colonel, who used to be a Major, is now a General.

MARY

(*Disinterestedly*)

Really?

CONOVER

He must be quite a guy.

MARY

He is.

CONOVER

Better keep in touch with him. Send him congratulations.

MARY

No, Jim. When he was a Major—I admit he was a major interest. But now, although he's a General, he's just a general interest.

(CONOVER *studies* MARY *for a minute.*)

199

CONOVER

Mary, you once spoke of a spanking as an indication of deep affection. There were some moments tonight when I could have turned you over my knee, but there wouldn't have been any affection in it.

MARY

All right, Jim. I'll agree I've behaved badly as a hostess. I'm not proud of my bad manners. But I'll bet you I'd be proud of what I said—if I could remember what I said.

CONOVER

(*Amused in spite of himself*)
You did let go some beauts.

MARY

Well, I think they're all stupid, selfish people.

CONOVER

I'd like to tell you how stupid I think you are. (*He goes to her*) Mary, I think it's time you were a little selfish, *and* a little intelligent. There's such a thing as enlightened self-interest you know. Why should you be stupid, just because Kay's being stupid?

MARY

Jim, that's one thing even I can't say about Kay—she's not stupid.

CONOVER

Isn't she? She's in there now doing her damnedest to get Grant into the White House. And the White House is the one place where she can't be with him. She can't follow him there, Mary. Have you ever thought of that?

MARY

(*Given pause*)

No, I hadn't.

CONOVER

Well, isn't it a little unintelligent of you to do anything to stop Grant from getting there? If he doesn't become President, I'm not so sure what's going to happen between you and him. But if he is elected—then you'll be the First Lady— in more ways than one.

MARY

(*Painfully*)

That doesn't necessarily follow.

CONOVER

I think it does—and I'll tell you why. I know how you feel toward Grant. You've never bothered to conceal it from me.

MARY

Okay. So I love him.

CONOVER

Mary, when I saw you and Grant in Detroit—before he spoke that night—there were two people in love. Maybe Grant hadn't said so—maybe Grant hadn't shown it in those little ways you were looking for—but if you had had another month alone together, you know what would have happened.

MARY
(*Not daring to believe it*)
I think you're wrong, Jim.

CONOVER
No, my dear, what he feels toward you goes pretty deep—
and I'll tell you how he gives himself away. It's in his respect
for your opinion—for what you think.

MARY
Don't kid me, Jim. We both know what happened to
Grant's speech on reconversion.

CONOVER
(*Sitting on the arm of her chair*)
Well, here's something you don't know—how unhappy
Grant is about that. He's good and sore at himself and I
know in my bones that some day what he thinks about reconversion—and Big Business—and what you think—is going to pop right out in the middle of a speech. I'm only
praying that it doesn't happen before the nomination, and
you'd better add a prayer, too.

MARY
But I want him to say it.

CONOVER
No, Mary! Not before the nomination! That's playing
Kay's game.

(SPIKE *enters.*)

SPIKE

Jim, can you come back in here? They're just breaking up.

CONOVER

I'll be there in a minute. (SPIKE *exits*) Mary, use your head. You can keep Grant from being President, but if you do, you're going to lose him. (*He rises*) Will you do something for me before I go tonight?

MARY

What?

CONOVER

I'd like to hear you say something to Grant that would let him know that if he does come our way just a little, you won't make life miserable for him. (MARY *is silent*) You're not the only one to be considered, Mary. Think of your children. That's a pretty good heritage—to be able to say, "My father was President of the United States."

MARY

Thanks, Jim. You're better than black coffee. You'd better get back in there.

CONOVER

(*Strolling toward the dining room*)

Oh, I'll hear it all later.

MARY

Oh, yes, Grant and Spike are going over to your hotel with you.

(CONOVER *stops in the arch and looks back at* MARY.)

CONOVER

No, Mary, we're going over to Mrs. Thorndyke's. (*He stands for a minute watching* MARY *who slowly turns and stares at him; then he exits.* MARY *sits thinking for a moment; then rises with determination and starts for the dining room but hears voices offstage and stops.*)

MRS. DRAPER

(*Offstage*)

Good night, everybody! (*She enters with* GRANT *and* HARDY) I'm sorry I have to run. I'm afraid I broke up the party.

GRANT

I'm sure you'll have time to get your train.

MRS. DRAPER

I have to stop at the hotel first. I'll get my wrap.

MARY

Can I help you?

MRS. DRAPER

No. I know right where it is. (*She exits into the powder room. The* SENATOR *and* CONOVER *enter but stay in the bar alcove talking together confidentially.*)

HARDY

(*To* MARY)

I'll say good night, Mrs. Matthews.

MARY

Good night. It was very nice having you here.

HARDY

(*To* GRANT)

I hope to hear from you on that.

GRANT

You'll be in touch with Jim.

HARDY

Just keep in mind what I said. Our funds are our secret weapon. If an employer knows how much we've got in the bank, he knows just how long we can stay out on strike. We can't afford to open our books.

GRANT

(*Smiling*)

As an employer I can understand that. Of course, I have to show my books.

HARDY

Well, good night. Good night, Mrs. Matthews. See you in Washington, Senator. (HARDY *exits.*)

SENATOR

(*Going to* MARY)

What you said about Sam Parrish—I can't wait to get back to Washington to tell it on him— (*Turns to* GRANT) Good night, Mr. Matthews— (*He draws him downstage*) Look, will you promise me this? Before you speak in the Middle West again, will you have another talk with me—and I'd like to have Ed O'Neal and Earl Smith there. We can handle the farm problems in Congress, but we'd like to be sure we won't run into any vetoes.

GRANT

(*Laughing*)

Vetoes! Senator, you're moving a little too fast for me. I haven't even started to work on my inaugural address.

MARY

(*Trying to take part*)

Inaugural address! My, that makes me nervous—and excited!

CONOVER

I'll be there holding your hand, Mary.

SENATOR

Jim, I know everything's safe in your hands. (*We hear a laugh from dining room*) Good night, Mr. Matthews. (*He shakes hands with* GRANT) Good night, Mrs. Matthews. (KAY *and* ALEXANDER *enter*) Good night, everybody! (SENATOR *exits.*)

KAY

I'll remember that, Judge, the next time I'm in New Orleans.

ALEXANDER

Where's Lulubelle?

MRS. DRAPER

(*Who has just entered with wrap*)

She's in the bedroom getting her things.

KAY

(*Crossing* MRS. DRAPER *downstage to door at left*)
I'd better get mine. (*She exits.*)

ALEXANDER

My coat is out there, isn't it? (*He indicates hall and exits into it.*)

MRS. DRAPER
(*Going to* MARY)
It was so nice meeting you, Mrs. Matthews.

MARY

Thank you. I hope we see each other soon.

MRS. DRAPER

You don't mind my falling in love with your husband, do you?

MARY

I don't see how you could help it.

MRS. DRAPER
(*To* GRANT)
I hope you and Jim get together on everything.

GRANT

Whoever the candidate is, you're going to be very valuable to him. I realize that.

(KAY *enters from the powder room with her wrap.*)

MRS. DRAPER

Well, if there's one group I do know how to swing, it's the foreigners. I don't pretend to be an intellectual, but since our so-called great minds have gotten us into the United Nations, we can't overlook the political advantage it gives us. Remember, there are lots of voters who are afraid of Russia!— And you'd be surprised how many people hate the British!

GRANT

I don't think we can capitalize on that, Mrs. Draper. We can't build world peace on hate. We have a certain leadership in the United Nations. We have to be very jealous of it.

KAY

Yes, but, Grant, if the Party's to win, remember each nationality in America will be thinking of their home country. We can use that. Am I right, Jim?

CONOVER

In Jersey City, Mayor Hague promised the Italians we'd rebuild Italy.

KAY

Exactly!

MRS. DRAPER

We've got to promise them that, and more, too!

CONOVER

It's bound to be part of the campaign. I don't see how we can very well avoid it. (*He has been eyeing* MARY) Do you, Mary?

MARY

(*Taking time to swallow*)

Well, some of the Democrats are being pretty open about it.

MRS. DRAPER

I do have to run. Good-bye, Mr. Matthews. You'll find I'm right about all this! (*She shakes hands with* GRANT. *To* MARY) Good night, Mrs. Matthews. It was a wonderful dinner—and such good talk! (*She crosses to the left arch and pauses to speak again to* MARY *who has followed her*) Of course my friends accuse me of thinking God is a Republican. But I'm fair-minded. I thank Him every night for Senator Bilbo. (MRS. DRAPER *and* MARY *exit together.* KAY *crosses to sofa and sits.* LULUBELLE *enters from the powder room, wearing her wrap.* JUDGE ALEXANDER *enters from the left arch, with his topcoat on, carrying his hat.*)

ALEXANDER

(*Crossing to* GRANT)

Mr. Matthews, I just happened to find in my overcoat pocket here a little pamphlet. It's a reprint of some of my most important decisions. I thought you might like to look it over. (*He hands pamphlet to* GRANT.)

GRANT

I'll be very glad to study it.

ALEXANDER

And I think I can safely promise you the votes of five Southern States.

GRANT
(Unbelieving)
In the election?

ALEXANDER
Hell, no!—In the convention! (*He crosses to the left arch.*)

LULUBELLE
Mr. Matthews, I can't tell you how crazy I am about that wife of yours. And that reminds me— (*She offers her hand to shake*) Congratulations!

GRANT
Congratulations? I don't think the Democrats have conceded yet.

LULUBELLE
No, I mean on your anniversary—your weddin' anniversary!

(GRANT *looks a bit blank, then it comes to him.*)

GRANT
(Shaking her hand vigorously)
Oh, yes, of course! Well, thank you!

(SAM *and* SPIKE *enter from the dining room.*)

SAM
Spike, I hate to bother you with it . . .

ALEXANDER
(*To* GRANT)

Remember, when you speak in New Orleans, you're going to be our house guest.

LULUBELLE

Good night, Mr. Matthews. But if you campaign through the South, you'd better change your name from Grant to Lee!

(LULUBELLE *and* ALEXANDER *exit through left arch.*)

SPIKE
(*To* CONOVER)

Jim, I'm going to try to switch Sam to your train tomorrow. You're on the Congressional, aren't you?

CONOVER

Yes.

SPIKE
(*To* SAM)

Better give me your space.

(SAM *hands* SPIKE *a railroad envelope.* SPIKE *sits down and makes notes on the envelope.*)

CONOVER

Yes, that's fine, Sam. I think on the way down we can have a pretty definite talk.

SPIKE

I'll get to work on it in the morning.

(MARY *enters from the left arch.*)

SAM

Well, I've got to catch up on my beauty sleep. Can I drop you, Mrs. Thorndyke?

GRANT

I'm going over to Jim's hotel with him. We can drop Mrs. Thorndyke. It's on the way.

SAM

Grant, the evening turned out fine. It was a great idea getting all these people together. Must have been something of an education for you. You see, Grant, you have to run your politics the same way you run your business. It's a question of taking practical measures.

(MARY *has come down to left of* SAM. CONOVER *is watching* MARY.)

GRANT

Sam, you'd better go home. You know you rile me. Pretty soon we'll be in an argument. (GRANT *gives* SAM *an affectionate push.*)

SAM

You're in a spot now where you can't indulge in any more of that radical talk. My God, look at the effect it's had on Mary!

GRANT

Sam, if you have nightmares, I'll bet they're all about Henry Wallace!

SAM

(*Remembering something*)

Oh, say!—Hilda'd never forgive me if I forgot to show you this. (*He takes a leather picture case from his pocket*) Look! It's Bobby, taken in Japan. Made a hell of a record—sixteen Jap planes.

GRANT

You must be very proud of Bobby.

SAM

He'll be out soon. He wants to go right into the business when he gets back. No more college. And I'm going to let him. Want to train him. I haven't got too many more years left. I want to leave him the soundest business in these whole United States. (*To* MARY *with almost pathetic justification*) That isn't anything to be ashamed of, is it, Mary?

MARY

(*Distressed*)

Give him my love when you write—and next time bring Hilda.

SAM

Good night, Mary. (*He kisses* MARY *and shakes hands with* GRANT.)

SPIKE

I'll leave your ticket at the hotel in the morning.

(JENNY *enters from the right arch with a tray.*)

SAM

See you on the train, Jim.

CONOVER

Good night, Sam.

(SAM *exits.*)

GRANT
(*To* JENNY)

Jenny, will you ask Swenson to bring down my coat? I left it upstairs.

(JENNY *exits and goes upstairs.* GRANT *goes to the ottoman and sits.*)

KAY

Spike, why don't you get Jim's coat?

(SPIKE *rises and starts for the left arch.* SWENSON *is seen going upstairs.*)

CONOVER

Well, Grant, you're still alive. I know you didn't look forward to this evening—but it wasn't so tough, was it?

GRANT

They certainly don't mind asking for heaven and earth, do they?

CONOVER

They don't expect to get heaven.

SPIKE

No, they'll settle for the earth. (SPIKE *exits into hall left.* MARY *sits on the arm of one of the chairs.*)

KAY

I was pretty frank with them. I told them there were some things they just couldn't ask Mr. Matthews to do. They were pretty reasonable—on the whole. Of course, there's no question about it—we'll have to meet them half way. (*She sees* GRANT *looking at her and smiles at him*) Part way, at least.

CONOVER

I'll get all these people alone. They know they can't get too tough with me. Of course there are some points we'll have to concede. We can't get through life without conceding some things, can we, Mary? (*He goes to* MARY *and puts his arm around her shoulder as if in reminder, but doesn't wait for an answer.* SPIKE *enters with* CONOVER's *coat*) I think all the Senator wanted to know was that Grant wouldn't fight the farm bloc. Hell, we all know we can't fight the farm bloc. They're too powerful.

(SPIKE *helps* JIM *into his coat.*)

GRANT

I'm afraid, Jim, that when it comes to concessions, the Senator and his crowd will have to make some. (SWENSON *enters with* GRANT's *coat and hat*) They want a floor under farm prices but no ceiling. They can't have it both ways.

CONOVER

Oh, there's always a margin of give and take. We won't
have any trouble there.

GRANT

(*Getting into his coat*)

Don't wait up, Swenson. I'm going to be late. (*He hands*
SWENSON *the* JUDGE's *pamphlet*) And throw this away, will
you? (*To the others*) Well, we'd better get going.

SPIKE

I don't think the Senator is going to be half as tough as
Mrs. Draper. I started kidding her. I said it was too bad we
couldn't dig up Hitler. There might be some votes in it. (*He*
chuckles) She didn't know whether I was on the level or
not. And from her answer, I don't know whether she was on
the level or not.

GRANT

(*Buttoning up his coat*)

If you ask me, I don't think she was kidding. I can't go
whole hog with her, Jim.

CONOVER

Of course she goes a little overboard—but you can't dismiss
the fact those issues are coming up, and we've got to find
some way of making a play for the foreign vote.

KAY

We know that every nation is going to feel the peace terms
have done them an injustice. We can make a perfectly honest

appeal for justice, and if that gets us some votes—I don't
think we should quibble.

GRANT

Which are you thinking of first, the votes or the justice?

CONOVER

Grant, we can't help ourselves! The Democrats are going
to play that side of the street—they're doing it already! Mary
agrees with us on that. (*He has been watching* MARY. *She,
instead of making any comment, rises and starts for the
stairway*) We can find some way to take a stand for justice
and still appeal to the foreign vote—and with a clear conscience. Don't you think so, Mary?

MARY

(*Turns*)

No! I don't! I tried to get out of the room before I got
sick, but you wouldn't let me! I've sat here listening to you
making plans for Grant to trade away the peace of the world
to get a few votes! Now that we're in the United Nations let's
use it—use it to get Italian votes and Polish votes—let's use
it to get the votes of those who hate the Russians and those
who hate the British! How long is it going to be before you
ask us to forgive Germany to get the German vote?

CONOVER

(*Warningly*)

Mary!

MARY

You heard Mrs. Draper and how much did it mean to you? "She's a little overboard"—"You can't quite go whole hog with her." And you heard Kay, too, cheering her on! None of you had the guts to tell them they are starting another war and to slap them down for it!

KAY

Now, Grant. Really!

CONOVER

Mary, do you know what you're doing?

MARY

Yes, Jim, I know what I'm doing! Look at Sam—he wants to leave a fortune to Bobby. What kind of a world is he going to leave to Bobby? The kind he wants isn't good enough for my children. Don't you know what's happened in the world? Are you willing to trust the people you brought here tonight with atomic power?

CONOVER

(*Harshly*)

We may not be as bright as you are, Mary, but the people here tonight were pretty representative.

MARY

Representative of what? Nobody represented the American people! They don't even represent the Republican Party. You represent what's dead in the Republican Party . . . and what's dead in the Democratic Party!

218

KAY

For Heaven's sake, Mary, have a little faith in Grant!

MARY

What have you got faith in? The people? You're afraid to let them know what Grant really thinks. Don't you believe in democracy?

KAY

(*Sharply*)

Why do you suppose we were here tonight? What do you think we were doing? All we were planning was the next election.

MARY

Yes, I know. Everybody here tonight was thinking of the next election. Well, it's time somebody began thinking of the next generation! (*She covers her face with her hands, sobbing, as she runs upstairs. There is a pause.*)

KAY

Well! . . . (*She turns to look at* GRANT. JIM *is also watching him.* GRANT *is standing in thought, without moving. There is another pause*) I think we could all use a drink. Let's go over to my house and go to work on some highballs. (*There is another pause as they wait for* GRANT *to break away from his thoughts.*)

CONOVER

Grace Draper will do what I tell her to do. But we have some things to settle. I want to be able to kid these people along.

GRANT

I'm not going to kid anybody along. I never have.

KAY

(*Pleadingly*)

Grant, everybody here tonight was thinking of the future
—which is how to get you elected. It's stupid right now to
think in any other terms.

(GRANT *unbuttons his coat and takes it off.* KAY *turns
to* CONOVER *in alarm.*)

CONOVER

(*Going to* GRANT)

Grant, I've got to talk to these people, and that means
you've got to talk to me!

GRANT

I'm talking to a lot of people in my speech Thursday night.
You'll be one of them. I promised myself when I went into
this that I'd appeal to the best in the American people. The
only advice I've ever had from any of you was to appeal to
their worst. And that's what both parties are starting to do
today. Let's end rationing! Who cares if Europe starves?
Let's lift price ceilings—suppose it does bring inflation. Let's
lower taxes and all get rich!

CONOVER

I see. You're the only honest man in politics.

GRANT

No, Jim! We have some damn good men! There are some wonderful men in the Senate and in the House, too—Democrats and Republicans. But damn it, Jim, there aren't enough of them to shape party policies. So, to get votes, both parties are out to buy the American public. I can't do that, Jim. So I'm afraid I can't be of any use to you.

(There is a slight pause.)

KAY

Well, Grant, I won't accept that decision. Oh, Grant, we've always talked these things out together. All right, we won't discuss it any more tonight. You're upset. I'll be in touch with you tomorrow. Come on, Jim. *(She starts to exit and turns back)* Be sure to tell Mary it was a charming evening. (KAY *exits.*)

CONOVER

I think Kay's right, Grant. You'd better sleep on it. I can stay over for another day.

GRANT

No, Jim. I've made up my mind.

CONOVER

Grant, you're wrong! In this country we play politics— and to play politics you have to play ball! (CONOVER *starts out.*)

GRANT

I'm sorry, Jim. I've become very fond of you.

CONOVER

Oh, don't send any flowers. It's not my funeral. (CONOVER *exits*.)

SPIKE

(*After a pause*)

Mr. Matthews, will you marry me?

GRANT

(*Laughing*)

Be careful, Spike, I'm in the mood for it! I've never felt so relieved in my life. Thank God, that's settled. I hope they're all listening in Thursday night! I'm going to burn their ears off. Any candidate for any office who threatens world peace for the sake of a few votes—there's the international criminal for you, Spike! I'll take care of them Thursday night—and from now on!

SPIKE

You know, Jim may have to take you on your own terms.

GRANT

No, Spike, it's all over but the shouting—but, oh, boy, am I going to shout! (GRANT *starts to take off his coat and roll up his shirt sleeves.* MARY *enters downstairs, is surprised to find* GRANT *and* SPIKE *there.* GRANT *pays no attention to her; he is busy with his thoughts.*)

MARY

I thought you were gone. Where's Jim?

SPIKE

I think he's cabling General MacArthur.

GRANT

(*Pacing*)

We've got to run business on a different basis . . .

MARY

What's happened?

SPIKE

Quiet, please, we're on the air.

GRANT

Sam and his type are dead! They want to go back to something they've had before. We've got to move on to something we've never had before. And I'm going to tell off the Senator, too. . . . (*Goes to* MARY) It's time somebody spoke up for the farmers. The American farmer is not the unpatriotic, selfish, grasping bastard the farm bloc makes him out to be! Thank God, I can speak my mind now— (*He looks back at* SPIKE) I don't have to worry about being a candidate!

SPIKE

Now you're on the beam. Talk as though you're not a candidate and I think they'll have to make you one.

GRANT

Forget it, Spike. (*He goes to* SPIKE *and shakes his hand*) It's been great working with you. But it's all over. I'll be seeing you. This isn't good-bye.

SPIKE

You're damn right it isn't good-bye. I'll be around first thing Friday morning. (*He starts out*) See you later, Mary.

GRANT

No, Spike, it's cold. But I'm in a great spot for my speech Thursday night. I haven't any commitments.

SPIKE

You've got one.

GRANT

What?

SPIKE

You promised not to make me Postmaster General. But I'll tell you what I'm doing, Grant—I'm releasing you from that. I'll be Postmaster General. (SPIKE *exits.*)

MARY

But, Grant, what happened?

GRANT

Mary, I'm not running for President. But that doesn't mean I'm out of politics. Nobody can afford to be out of politics. I'm going to be yelling from the sidelines; you've got to be yelling; everybody's got to be yelling! I'm going to be in there asking questions, and I'm going to see that the people get the answers!

MARY

There are a lot of questions to ask, Grant. You're going to be a busy man.

GRANT

You're damned right I'll be busy. Say, I didn't do a real job in any one of my plants. Let's make the trip all over again.

MARY

But, Grant, you need a rest first. We both do.

GRANT

All right. What do you say we go back to Victoria?

MARY

Victoria?

GRANT

Say—do you know something? (*He crosses to* MARY, *shaking finger at her*) You forgot this is our wedding anniversary!

MARY

(*Pretending surprise*)
I did? Oh, damn it all to hell!

(GRANT *gives* MARY *a resounding smack on the behind.*)

GRANT

Cut that out, Maizie! (*The realization comes to* MARY *that he has smacked her and called her "Maizie." Her face slowly lights up.* GRANT *continues pacing and talking to* MARY *and the world*) I've got to get back to work! We've all got to get back to work! There is a big job ahead for all of us! (*He stops and looks at* MARY *and then goes to her*) Darling, you're right about the future. We've got something great to work for! (*He reaches* MARY *and takes her in his arms.*)

Curtain